Poet's Guide

POET'S GUIDE

How to Publish and Perform Your Work

Michael J. Bugeja

Story Line Press
1995

Published by Story Line Press, Three Oaks Farm, Brownsville, OR 97327

This publication was made possible thanks in part to the generous support of the Nicholas Roerich Museum, the Andrew W. Mellon Foundation, the National Endowment for the Arts, and our individual contributors.

Book design by Chiquita Babb

Library of Congress Cataloging-in-Publication Data

Bugeja, Michael J.
    Poet's guide : how to publish and perform your work / Michael J. Bugeja.
        p.   cm.
    Includes index.
    ISBN 1-885266-00-6
    1. Poetry—Marketing.   2. Oral interpretation of poetry.
I. Title
PN1059.M3B84   1995
808.1—dc20   95-36577
                                            CIP

Contents

Chapter Three

Chapter Four

Chapter Seven

Permissions

"After the Argument" is reprinted with the permission of Judi K. Beach.

"Hearing With My Son" by Stephen Corey originally appeared in *Synchronized Swimming* published in 1985 by Swallow's Tale Press and reprinted in 1993 by Livingston University Press.

The two drafts of "Fatherly Love: The Obsession" and related correspondence are reprinted with the permission of Joan Halperin.

"Half Spring" is reprinted with the permission of R. Nikolas Macioci.

"On Fading to Invisible" is reprinted with the permission of Marion Brimm Rewey.

The two drafts of "We Who Can Never Find Our Glasses" are reprinted with the permission of Betty Shipley.

"There is a Streak of Quiet Melancholy" by Eve Shelnutt originally appeared in *Recital in a Private Home,* published in 1990 by Carnegie Mellon University Press.

Preface

As poetry columnist for *Writer's Digest,* editor of two *Poet's Market* directories, and author of *The Art & Craft of Poetry,* I answer practical questions from authors each day—as many as fifty letters per month. Although the questions vary, most concern how to find an audience for their work or how to remove obstacles keeping them from finding an audience.

Some are from beginners like this Michigan poet who writes: "As a child, I was drawn to poetry—reading, writing, listening. I've been writing poetry since I was a teen. For many years every poem I wrote ended up in the trash, because of the fear of letting that personal side of me be known. In the last seven years I have accumulated 40 poems and have just started to share them with friends and family. . . . My dream is to get them published. I have not the slightest idea of how to start."

Others are from more seasoned poets who have experienced difficulties trying to place poems with magazines. Typically these writers have made a serious commitment to poetry, investing in reference books and computer equipment; some even have begun to publish in small-press and literary magazines. But often they run into unanticipated problems like this Arizona poet who writes: "One thing you have yet to touch on is what to do when magazines do not respond to your submission. For reasons unknown to me, a large percentage of the magazines I have been submitting to over the past year have not responded. What is our recourse then?"

Occasionally I get letters from well-known poets who want to schedule more readings or who wonder how to sell more of their books. One creative writing professor with four collections to his credit asks: "How do I reach a popular audience . . . without giving the appearance of 'selling out?'" Another poet who has published more than forty poems in top journals is frustrated because he cannot find a book publisher. He asks: "Should I self-publish?" Another poet has relocated to Israel and confides, "Because of the out-of-the-way place I live, I do not have easy access to libraries. What I would like to know from you, if you would, is a short list of some basic books on writing and marketing poetry."

I answered these writers and filed their letters with others in a cardboard box under my desk. (I have four full boxes in my closet.) One day I waded through them letter by letter, debating whether to keep or dispose of them, when I discovered that readers tended to ask the same questions. Although circumstances differed, poets were seeking advice on submitting poems, joining workshops, attending conferences, doing readings, entering contests, dealing with editors, and assembling, publishing, and selling their books.

I started grouping these letters into files. Soon those files suggested a book—the one you are reading—a comprehensive text that would contain information on publishing and performing poetry, and guide beginning and experienced poets to ever larger audiences for their work.

Marketing is vital if you want to reach an audience, but few "experts" want to discuss it. I know that I never learned much about placing poetry when I studied creative writing at Oklahoma State University. The talented writers there would showcase their poems, stories, articles, and books in glass cabinets and the graduate students would admire the wares. Publishing your work was important, it seemed. But *talking* about publishing your work was, somehow, tacky.

Our oracle of marketing info was a pile of coffee-stained literary magazines in the conference room. We were supposed to read them and figure it all out. Sometimes poets passed through and gave readings. I attended many of them. Once I saw Fred

Chappell receive a standing ovation because he delivered his work so well. Occasionally grad students gave readings, reciting their poems too fast, flubbing their lines. Sometimes these same students would work months polishing their work for a reading that few people attended because the students did not publicize the event. But no professor wanted to discuss how to give good readings and attract an audience. We were supposed to go to readings and learn on our own. The skill, apparently, would come with time and experience.

We had contests, too. Each year a student would win an Academy of American Poets university prize or an Oklahoma State University Fiction Prize. These were coveted awards. Winners were recognized as rising stars in the program (and also received a little cash). But it was positively taboo to inquire about *how* to win either of these awards because "good work speaks for itself" (especially when nobody's talking).

Finally we were supposed to assemble our best poems in book form to meet our thesis or dissertation requirements. There was no handbook for that, either. You met with and relied on your advisor for such advice and hoped that he or she was not fighting with anyone else on your committee or had taken another job before you had your defense. If so, you faced the possibility of the assembly of poems changing again to suit the opposing committee member or the new advisor.

In sum, I had to learn most of what I know about marketing by trial and error. I don't recommend the method. It costs time and wastes money and supplies, and annoys editors and the public. Worse, you might mistakenly believe that publishers dislike your poetry or that you lack the talent to make a name for yourself in the literary world. You could become so discouraged that you stop submitting poetry. You could get writer's block, a tricky infection.

You may be beyond that point already. You survived. Maybe you've been publishing poetry regularly in decent magazines. Your problem now is getting a book accepted. You'll need that book, too, especially if you hope to teach poetry one day at a university. The longer you keep sending your manuscript to the wrong publisher, the longer you'll dwell in T.A. hell. Or you may have published a chapbook or book, but your second collection is languishing on the shelf. Maybe your first book sold *ten* copies—I know someone's who did!—and you can't figure out why your publisher won't take your latest tome. Well, if you don't know how to publicize and promote your work—which, by the way, *doesn't* speak for itself—you might falsely label yourself as just another poetaster . . . and jettison your dreams.

I've been through all of those stages. I got discouraged when I was rejected because I didn't know how to send out my work. I had published 186 poems before I placed my first book. And that was in England. Then I stopped believing that good work speaks for itself. I realized that good work speaks for itself *in front of the right editor.* So I boned up. I bought some directories, sent away for guidelines, bought sample copies of magazines that published poems like mine. I asked book publishers what they were looking for and explained how I could help deliver it, along with hundreds of readers. That's one of the reasons I landed the columnist job at *Writer's Digest* and took over the reins for two years at *Poet's Market* after its creator Judson Jerome passed away in August 1991. I wasn't the only poet being considered as Jerome's successor. But I knew more about publishing: how to put together a strong manuscript, effectively present the poetry to an audience at a public reading or slam, deal professionally with editors, and assemble and publish chapbooks and books.

Poet's Guide contains this and more information and advice that seldom appears in poetry texts or is taught in writing programs:

- *Workshops.* You can find articles in the library about joining a creative writing workshop in an English department. But you'll turn up little information on organizing private workshops or selecting conference ones. You'll encounter all that in Chapter One, with advice and insight from poets Diane Wakoski of the University of Michigan and Roger Jones of Southwest Texas State University.

- *Poetry Readings.* Scheduling a poetry reading is one thing. Organizing, publicizing, and performing it is another (especially in an era of open mikes, cafe slams, TV and cable presentations.) In Chapter Two, you'll get some practical advice on such matters. Better yet, Nancy Kress and Karen Joy Fowler—two excellent readers I met at the Brockport Writers' Forum in New York—will help you prepare for and overcome problems that crop up during performances.

- *Contests.* In Chapter Three, you'll analyze the winning entries and ways of such poets as Stephen Corey, associate editor at *The Georgia Review,* and R. Nik Macioci, Marion Brimm Rewey, and Judi K. Beach. I'll introduce various types of literary contests and explain how to gather marketing information on each one to gain the inside track.

- *Publishing.* In case you don't know, the publishing process entails more than sending out manuscripts and waiting for replies. You have to type or print poems in a standard format, write cover letters, keep records, deal with editors, sign contracts, compose bio notes, proof galleys and more. To help you wade through it, I've developed a step-by-step process in Chapter Four.

- *Revising for Publication.* This is perhaps the most critical element of marketing (also seldom, if ever, discussed). Say you have an editor interested in your work at a magazine in which you always hoped to publish, but he or she wants you to revise your poem first. What to do? Chapter Five focuses on that. You'll read actual rewrite requests from editors of such literary magazines as *TriQuarterly,* illustrated by original and revised versions of individual poems.

- *Assembling Collections.* This is another basic but important chapter, especially if you're a grad student in a creative writing program. Here you'll learn how to compile chapbooks and books. You'll encounter three types—narrative, lyric, combined—and see how these formats require different assemblies. You'll also find information about typing and format requirements.

- *Publishing Collections.* The last chapter emphasizes ways to research and select publishers and identifies various publishing options. You'll learn how to negotiate a contract for a book and how to promote the published product so that it reaches as many readers as possible.

In addition to the information in each chapter, I added another level of instruction by inviting prestigious creative writers to give their perspectives and advice. You'll read comments on each of the chapter topics from Neal Bowers, longtime editor of *Poet & Critic*; Andrea Hollander Budy, Nicholas Roerich award-winning poet; Jim Barnes, editor of *Chariton Review* and writer-in-residence at Northeast Missouri State University; Fred Chappell, winner of the Bolligen Prize and poetry reviewer for *The Georgia Review*; Kelly Cherry, novelist, poet and creative writing professor at the University of Wisconsin-Madison; David Citino, director of Ohio State University Press; Ruth Daigon, editor of *Poets On*; Lucia Cordell Getsi, Capricorn Award winner and editor of *Spoon River Poetry Review*; Lola Haskins, winner of the Piper Award at the University of Iowa Press; Jonathan Holden, nationally known critic and poet and winner of the Juniper Prize; Colette Inez, award-winning poet, gifted reader, and beloved workshop leader; Judith Kitchen, poet and essayist, reviewer for *The Georgia Review* and editor of State Street Press; Susan Ludvigson, esteemed writer and educator; R.T. Smith, co-editor of *Southern Humanities Review*; Laurel Speer, critic and frequent writer's conference speaker; Leonard Trawick, editor, Cleveland State Poetry Center; and Ron Wallace, poetry book editor and distinguished poet.

My goal is to give you information and encouragement so that you bring the joy of poetry to more people. I have tried to include something for everyone in *Poet's Guide*—even a glossary of literary and publishing terms used in the text that a new poet might not yet know. I've also added marketing exercises geared to your personal level of development: beginning, intermediate, advanced. This will keep you focused as a poet, enabling you to set goals for yourself and share your work with an ever-expanding audience.

Finally, *Poet's Guide* can be used in tandem with standard textbooks like my *Art and Craft of Poetry* (Writer's Digest Books) or directories like *Poet's Market*, providing you with all you need to know about publishing, promoting, and performing your verse.

Michael J. Bugeja
Athens, Ohio

Poet's Guide

Chapter One

Joining a Workshop

As a young writer, I was a solo operator. My workshop was my bookshelf, and the library's bookshelf. And I don't regret it. My passion to please might have driven me either to give up or to turn into someone I wasn't. . . . In balance I think that as long as you don't fall into the trap of losing yourself by trying to please other people, and that's a trap much bigger than any writing workshop, I think that heeding informed advice, under controlled circumstances, can be a really productive thing to do

—Lola Haskins

Introduction to Workshops

THE WORD "WORKSHOP" is most often associated with creative writing programs at universities, but the term is much more comprehensive than that. In essence, a workshop is any place where writers gather—from cafes to conferences—to critique and improve their verse. Workshops can be as varied and enriching as the people who belong to or lead them. Typically they include as few as three poets or as many as twenty; are conducted at schools, conference sites, public facilities, or homes; and feature a "leader" who sets the goals or groundwork for such sessions.

The real role of a workshop, however, is an implied commitment. A poet decides that he or she will improve as a writer so that one day an editor will accept poems for publication. Even poets who claim to compose solely to please themselves understand this on some level, or they wouldn't have joined a workshop. Thus, the decision to participate with others in critique sessions actually is the first step in a long, complex process of reaching an audience.

Nonetheless, the workshop model can be difficult to embrace. In the past, according to literary myth, the great masters worked alone and honed their immortal styles without too much outside interference. (Indeed, it is humorous to imagine Walt Whitman leading a writing workshop or Emily Dickinson enrolling in one.) But it is also true that Wordsworth had his Coleridge and Eliot had his Pound and poets of all ages have asked other poets to critique their verse so that they could convey their truths with greater impact or appeal. So all a workshop is, then, is a convenient way for poets to meet and work with other writers at regular intervals.

Types of Workshops

Basically, there are four:

1. *Creative Writing Workshop.* This type has been developed by English departments with creative writing sequences and usually features a successful, knowledgeable poet at the helm. Often, to join such a workshop, you have to be a student enrolled in a particular college (although some colleges allow non-students to audit workshops). If a college or university in your area offers such a workshop, and you are not a student, check with the Registrar to see if you can audit the class or simply ask the poet for permission to participate.

2. *Community Workshop.* Because many colleges do not allow non-students to enroll in creative writing workshops, or because non-students work during the day and cannot afford to audit them, many communities offer workshops at night through schools, churches, or recreation centers. Contact administrators of such facilities and ask if they (a) offer a community workshop, (b) know of any, or (c) would be willing to sponsor one. (If an administrator agrees to sponsor a workshop, give him or her a copy of this chapter and help organize, lead, or otherwise promote the sessions.)

3. *Writing Conference Workshop.* This type of group is part of a writing conference featuring craft sessions, visiting poets, and readings. Usually such literary events are organized around a workshop that lasts the better part of a week or even a month. To locate such a workshop, read freelance magazines like *Writer's Digest* or *Poets & Writers Magazine* that contain advertisements for summer or fall conferences. Or join a state poetry society or writing federation and attend that annual conference.

4. *Private Writing Workshop.* As its name also implies, this type of workshop is one that you or another poet organize and that meets at your or another poet's home. Many writers like personal workshops because they are more informal than other kinds or more flexible. (For instance, you may want to organize one that focuses only on political poetry or that promotes only formal verse.) To arrange one, contact friends and/or associates who also compose poetry or put out a call for poets by placing ads or personals in local media. Set a convenient time and, if you like, ask members to bring snacks or dishes for a potluck after the work has been done.

No matter how appealing a workshop may seem at first blush, you should know the benefits and drawbacks of each type. Let's start with the creative writing workshop, usually led by productive poets. They have to be because competition for these jobs is keen and, to earn tenure or promotion, professors have to publish. Thus, they should be well-read and in-the-know about literary trends. Moreover, their workshops often are highly structured; for example, students should receive course outlines that detail what needs to be accomplished to earn a good grade.

On the minus side, professors often promote styles that are trendy, resulting in a "workshop" poem that focuses overmuch on language skills—the executed metaphor, the learned symbol, the open ending—rather than on insight, experience, or truth. Because grades or careers are at stake, students often have similar goals or ambitions, resulting in a desire to please the instructor (by citing books the student has read or name-dropping in general) rather than by concentrating on the work in question.

The quality of instruction may vary from excellent to poor at community writing workshops. Depending on the instructor, usually paid a nominal fee to lead the sessions, the structure of a workshop can be too casual becauses grades are not at stake. Consequently, lesser standards are upheld. Sometimes looser structures and lesser standards result in flexibility and freedom to explore styles and discover new ones. Sometimes this results in chaos. You may want to enroll in a community workshop to meet people who have unusual backgrounds or significant experiences. Occasionally, however, such participants do not take the art and craft of poetry seriously; for them, it is a mere hobby, much like archery or French cooking. When too many such people enroll in a community workshop, the quality of critiques suffers.

A workshop at a writing conference features top-name poets. Quality of instruction usually is excellent. These poets augment incomes by leading workshops around the country and so try to impress conference-goers who pay dearly to attend such events. Often you can sit down with such a poet in individual critique sessions—a privileged honor. Moreover, because such a workshop is conducted during many other scheduled events at a conference, sessions can be highly structured and critiquing tough and thorough. (After all, in a day or two, the star poet will be on his or her way out of town and figures you might as well get your money's worth.) Because participants pay fees and travel to conference sites, they, too, are motivated; thus, sessions are often extraordinarily productive. But the drawbacks of such workshops are obvious, too: they are expensive and short. Usually all that a poet can afford is one per year, and that is hardly enough to polish a year's worth of work.

On the other hand, at no cost, you can schedule as many private workshops as you desire. They can last all year, too. The benefits here are obvious as well: you'll be working with poets you like and who will motivate and support you, celebrating your sales and success as if they were their own. The drawbacks are equally obvious: you'll lack a workshop leader or one of you will assume that role, and that can be deemed unfriendly or pretentious. Personal critiques from people you know may sting more than they would if received from strangers in a public or an academic setting. Worse, the structure of private sessions can be so loose or social that sometimes you won't even conduct a workshop, partying, arguing, or celebrating instead.

If you know the benefits and drawbacks of each type of workshop, you will be better able to select ones that appeal to you or improve ones that don't. To help you in this process, let's see what goes on—or should go on—during these sessions.

The Standard Workshop

Each workshop should have four components:

1. *You have to write.* If you join a workshop, you should compose new poems rather than submit final drafts of old ones to the group. Many poets cheat, pretending that their final drafts are first ones to impress the leader and participants or to lessen the odds of receiving harsh critiques. Resist that temptation. You will be relieved to learn that the first drafts of other poets are as messy or convoluted as your own. Don't try to curry favor with the leader or other poets, either, by writing in a style that pleases them or plays up to *their* political or personal agendas.

This is *your* workshop. Use it to increase your productivity, to hone your style, or to convey your truths. If your style is inept and your truths, improper, they will become even more so if you abandon them and pretend you are someone else. Conversely, the more you write, the more you will discover the true nature of your style and/or convictions. Finally, make sure your workshop leader allows you to compose in a tradition that interests or challenges you. If you like rhyme and meter, for instance, and your workshop leader doesn't, demand that he or she critique you by upholding standards of that style. The same rule applies if you like free or avant-garde verse, and your workshop leader doesn't. In sum, it is the *leader's* responsibility to adapt to the various styles of poetry to help participants achieve their potential.

2. *You have to critique.* Make a goal to give better than you get, because if you learn to criticize the work of others so that they may improve their writing, ultimately you will benefit. You will know more about craft and that will help you compose better poems. Your first impulse may be to help another poet revise his or her work only to the point that it is still inferior to your own. Resist that temptation, too. Help others make poems that exceed your standards, and soon your standards will be raised and the quality of your verse enhanced.

Compete only with yourself. Just as you shouldn't write to please people in a workshop or alter your own style of verse or convictions to appease them, neither should you expect others to write the way you do or to believe in your convictions. Instead, if you like to write experimental poems and have to critique a sonnet (or vice versa), criticize the work for what it is rather than what it can be. You'll learn about poetry and criticism in the process. Likewise if you believe in equality for all people and have to critique what you consider a racist or sexist poem, don't attack the poet and provoke a counterattack when your work is being considered. Instead, either refrain from criticizing the work and acknowledge that your own beliefs make it impossible for you to do so objectively, or focus on the voice of a work and suggest it be less arrogant in tone or more compassionate. Don't worry. If verse is unenlightened, others will know it intuitively and good editors will never accept it for publication. That, in itself, should make you feel easier.

3. *You have to read.* In many workshops you will be asked to read books of contemporary poetry. In others, contemporary criticism. And in a few, a textbook about contemporary poetry and/or criticism in addition to an overview of verse from other eras. Occasionally you will do all three in addition to composing poems and giving critiques.

In large part, this will depend on the type of workshop that you have joined. Reading usually is mandatory in an academic workshop and encouraged in a community one. Because poets and other writers sell their books at conferences, reading is a implied component here, too. Of course, the beauty of private workshops is the loaning of books among friends. In general, aspiring poets seldom read as many poetry books as they should and rarely check out criticism or textbooks in the library. Reading poetry can help inspire your muse, illustrate how elements of craft are applied in a work, or generally enlighten you. Reading criticism and poetry texts will help you give good critiques during workshop.

Finally, don't depend on the requirements of a workshop to read books about poetry, criticism, and instruction. If your workshop lacks a reading component, institute one on your own, looking up text books and anthologies in the library and later the books of poets and critics whose names or works are mentioned or included in these publications. Or ask your workshop leader or participants to lend you their books and do likewise, trading and keeping track of collections so you can reclaim and return them later.

4. *You have to keep a journal.* Keeping journals usually is a requirement in an academic workshop. Simply, you will be asked to read books and write about them in your journal and then you will hand in your journals so the professor can ascertain whether you have understood the assignment. Keeping journals in other types of workshops usually is optional. I recommend it

without reservation but with these stipulations: whenever you read a book, bracket the best excerpts in pencil and then copy those passages in your journal, along with your feelings about them; finally, at the end of each session, record the highlights (and lowlights) when you give and get critiques. Such a personal log will indicate your own growth over time as a poet and critic and provide you with an outlet to vent your frustrations or express your elations (or otherwise put the workshop into perspective).

To help you decide which type of workshop might best appeal to you, in upcoming sections of this chapter I'll illustrate the kind of tough and thorough critique you might get in an individual critique session at a writer's conference. Then I'll call on poets who have different perspectives about workshops. Finally, I'll summarize reasons why you should consider joining one, so that you can decide for yourself.

Tough Critique

On average, I keynote about four poetry conferences per year. Though I enjoy meeting poets, I take the individual workshop sessions seriously and critique poems vigorously. Personally, I think too many well-known poets spend a minute or two scanning a draft and then ad-lib during such sessions, praising the conference-goer because this is what they think he or she wants to hear. Maybe.

Most conference-goers I have met are serious about poetry. They don't mind enduring 20 to 30 minutes with a critiquer who is going to tell the truth, point out strengths (and weaknesses) and provide practical advice.

At a recent conference, I met several poets who were confident about their abilities. One of them—Betty Shipley, poetry columnist for the freelance magazine *Byline*—allowed me to share my critique of her work. Shipley has a reputation as a tough workshop leader, herself. She's an adjunct professor of poetry at the University of Central Oklahoma and author of two chapbooks, the most recent being *Somebody Say Amen* (Pointriders Press). After her session, Shipley told me: "I know you spent a lot of time and mental effort to make something better of our poems—more time than we spent writing them, I'd say. I know how tempting it is to just respond 'that's nice' . . . or point out the best in a lot of awful. That is all some poets want."

Not Shipley. Her poem and my suggested revision appear below. Read the poems and then I'll make some observations.

The Original Draft:

We Who Can Never Find Our Glasses

We who can never find our glasses see the world
more lovely, jagged edges rounded neatly
imperfections smoothed into beauty. We pass smirk
and scowl simplified into smile and anything
not accompanied by harsh words flips right on by.

Fall for us is weeks late among the hazy green, and spring
arrives small and unnoticed then bursts into sight
like an accident. After dark on misty nights we are happily lost in

ribbons of neon and common street lamps hazed in halos
or fractured into spiders of light. We look up, and cosmic fender-
benders drop out entirely. We promote fireflies to supernovas, and if
there is snow we are often found helpless and babbled
in light and beauty. We who can never find our glasses

have no snakes in our grass. We miss bears in the woods. Forests
and jungles are swallowed whole in our eyes without wolves or tigers.
No buildings need paint or urban neighborhoods renewal.
Alleys slip by in volumes of dark and whole cities smear into horizon.

Until we find our glasses things escape us. All letters are good news
and no sign points except the way we want to go. But sad to say
we who can never find our glasses are often accompanied

by those who don't need them and are too willing to interpret
and correct. The clusters of white flowers lining the highway
for miles on that moonscape of Chihuahua Desert were reduced to
    Pampers
used and blown permanently into cacti, and those white tulips
in the yard of the house on Sooner Road so mysteriously early
against the uncanny green—Tampax leached of blood and magic;
blooms forced and impelled not by Dylan's "green fuse" but by a
    faulty
septic system. It makes the person who can never find her glasses
want new friends or contact lenses.

⌒

The Critiqued Draft:

Vision

We who lose our glasses find the world
more lovely, jagged edges rounded,
imperfections smoothed to beauty. We pass smirk
and scowl as smile, contented:

Fall comes weeks late, hazy green; spring,
small, unnoticed, then aburst
like an accident.
               After dark in mist

we ease into ribbons of neon and halos of streetlamps,
fractured spiders of light. We look up
as fireflies go nova. Whole cities smear into horizon
until the Samaritan restores us, interprets:

The clusters of white flowers on that moonscape
of Chihuahua Desert, mere Pampers
blown into cacti, blooms impelled not
by Dylan's "green fuse" but by mind's Degas impressions.

As you can see, I took out my red pen and cut, cut, cut. Betty
Shipley admits that the original draft was, as she puts it, "so

visually dense on the page that it discouraged me. I could never decide which images should be cut in all that sprawl." Though I admired many of the images in her work, I also knew that the poem would gain power only if the *best* images were kept in a subsequent draft. In addition, some phrases were plain wordy—"After *dark* on misty *nights,*" for example. Moreover, the idea behind the poem did not justify a lyric of this length. Before I showed her my revision during our critique session at the conference, I told her: "The idea here is wonderful but you need to take it more seriously. Your goal is to *show* us that the world is lovely in our myopic haze, but you tell us too often. The idea needs to startle, as vision startles. You need to condense and rise above the ordinary, especially in the ending."

Some individual critiques will end there. If I did this, however, I would have been commiting the same mistake as a critiquer that I was accusing Shipley of as a poet. In sum, I would have been *telling* her what was wrong with her poem instead of *showing* her how to correct it. That's why I excised so many lines and phrases—more than 200 words, to be exact. I added fewer than 25 to stitch the poem together. Although I lost several good images—"babbled in light and beauty," for instance—the remaining images melded to empower the piece. Says Shipley, "I brought the poem to my poetry class thinking when they saw your marks, they might feel better about what I do to theirs. They seemed quite cheered by the sheer presence of so much red."

Shipley also knows the two cardinal rules about surviving an individual critique session at a conference:

Listen to what the commentator recommends but take only as much advice as you need.

If a critiquer gives you a word or a line—or an entire revised poem—take it, especially if you're paying for it at a conference. Gifts are rare in this business.

"I was delighted with your close editing," Shipley says. "The poem has lost no magic. I miss the Tampax scene only because it really happened and I have never made so laughable a judgment—no reason at all to burden a poem with it, though."

Shipley's remarks show that her poem is more important than her pride. She was open to intense criticism. Likewise, I knew that we would have fewer than 30 minutes for me to make a lasting impression on her. That's the dynamic of an individual workshop at a conference. This can differ greatly from the kind you will find in a creative writing program, however.

Other Perspectives

Diane Wakoski and Roger Jones teach at major universities. Jones is a poet and personal friend who attended workshops with me while we were in college and who helped me organize a private one. Wakoski, a well-known and widely published poet, is a no-nonsense, craft-oriented critic.

Says Jones: "I remember the workshop we were in (with T.R. Hummer as leader), and got a good bit out of that one. Much of that had to do with Hummer, of course, who really understands the chemistry of poetic lines, and who helped me to approach each poem by critiquing what its writer has set up as the poem's obstacles. Hummer also had a rather remarkable ability to strip poems down and rebuild them, playing different lines off each other, making new and interesting entities. The class itself was an interesting one, too, with a good bit of diversity. I think more than anything, that class helped me to learn to locate certain pockets of energy in my otherwise flaccid language and to follow the impulses of those areas of energy. It also helped me learn to wrestle more with cliches, my biggest adversary in writing.

"But I have mixed feelings about workshops overall, since they don't always accomplish much, and since it is often very tempting for a young writer simply to veer off in the direction of his or her mentor's opinions, or to write like that person, as happened with me. Also the workshop often tends to encourage a 'publication first' mentality, and the writer ends up modeling poems to suit current magaazine trends rather than to encounter vital parts of self and experience.

"On the whole, I have come to believe that writing poetry is largely a solitary matter. Two of the things I have learned that have been especially valuable to me have been rather recent solitary discoveries: the richness that comes with revising, and the need to lower my often severe standards. I keep an inch-thick file nowadays with poem drafts, beginnings and misfires—maybe as many as fifty drafts of things, most of which will never see print, many of which are utterly terrible—and I move back and forth, working a line here and there, just watching over it all and letting the better work 'steep.'

"As for private workshops, there are probably a dozen or so non-academic writing groups where I live, most of which got going, I think, largely by word of mouth, and around clusters of like-thinking friends. Some advertise in little newspapers, bringing in people from the outside. Some are very successful and a few promote certain types of poetry—preachy environmental and anarchist Beat-type stuff, for instance.

"Then again, private writing groups are easy to crank up. We've had an on-again, off-again one here. Right now it's off-again but there is talk about starting it up. Sometimes it's hard for me to try to seine the good constructive criticism from the stylistic biases of the participants. That seems to be the major problem with workshops in general, however, on or off campus."

Diane Wakoski's approach deviates from Jones' and from the standard concept of what a workshop should be. Hers does not put the burden on participants to provide the bulk of criticism, with the leader moderating and evaluating discussion. She takes a more active role.

According to Wakoski: "In a good workshop, you are receiving information about the way others perceive your poems. You probably won't do this on your own. On their own, most people won't develop a strong enough critical awareness to be able to see what is weak or wrong, though reading well-written poems is the best way to get information about how to improve your writing. Therefore, the kind of poetry workshop I believe in and offer is one where I am the sole critic, where each poem is analyzed for mythic content and successful use of figurative language, and where it is mercilessly scrutinized for language that is careless, imprecise, sentimental, cliched or melodramatic.

"The benefit of this kind of workshop is that students learn to think rigorously about their poems. Even if they do not accept my judgments totally, they become aware of how I see their work and thus begin to have a greater awareness of how others might also perceive it.

"The danger of workshops in general is that personality overshadows the writing on the page and can lead to the belief that if people could just meet you and understand you, they would think your poetry is good. Poems have to stand on their own, once they are published. A good workshop makes you aware of the voice which your poems begin to have collectively, and it teaches you to work on that voice, to develop your personal mythology in the poems, so that finally you don't have to speak up for your poems.

"They speak eloquently for you."

Workshop Checklist

Now that you have become acquainted with the various types of workshops and the benefits and drawbacks of each, let's end with a list summarizing reasons why you might want to join one:

1. *To enter an MFA or creative writing program.* Often a degree-granting program will require you to send a manuscript with your application for admittance. So you may want to join a private, community, or conference workshop to compose and polish new verse.

2. *To increase productivity.* Like it or not, workshops force you to work, so if you are having trouble generating new poems, this may be the vehicle to help you overcome any writing blocks.

3. *To sharpen the rewriting process.* In a workshop, you not only produce more poems but also critique more than you normally would. You focus on "what works" and "what doesn't work," emphasizing craft. This alone will hone your rewriting abilities.

4. *To toughen your muse.* If you have trouble receiving criticism, or criticizing the work of others, you will learn one important thing in a workshop: to put aside your ego and put the poem first.

5. *To appreciate structure.* The best workshops are ones in which participants know what is expected of them. So much is accomplished in so short a time that you will end up organizing your own time better when you are working at home.

6. *To read more books.* The best workshops are ones in which reading is emphasized, exposing you to different styles of poetry and applications of craft.

7. *To measure the impact of your work.* If you are unsure about your poems, a workshop may be an ideal place to discover the effectiveness of experimental verse or new personal styles.

8. *To reflect on your work.* Normally poets produce and send out manuscripts, judging their worth by the number of acceptances that they receive. This can be a faulty barometer because publication can be fickle. In a workshop, however, someone usually will challenge your beliefs so that you find yourself having to defend them. Later you will reflect on the experience to put it—and your work—into perspective.

9. *To meet people of similar or different backgrounds.* You'll be motivated by poets who share your beliefs, affected by others who don't, and intrigued by ones from diverse social, ethnic, or regional heritage.

10. *To make contacts.* You'll meet workshop leaders who have influence in the poetry world. If you are serious and do good

work, they will be glad to claim you as a student and may help you target magazines or even introduce you to editors.

Guidebook

Judith Kitchen's Workshop Guidelines

I've been teaching writing workshops for quite some time now and have been on the other end of the process when, as an adult student, I worked for my MFA in poetry.

In years of observing workshops, I've seen every possible type of participant from the vocal critic to the silent listener. I believe the workshop setting has something to offer almost every type of writer as long as he or she can maintain personal integrity. There's also the danger that the heady atmosphere and camaraderie can become addictive. You then become "a workshop junkie."

Most of writing takes place in solitude and is generated by a singular point of view. I think it's best to work alone for a time, then use a workshop as a place to touch base with an audience. A "group" is slightly different from a more formal workshop such as a summer workshop or a college class; a group is local, regular, something you can come to count on. A group offers you support, sustenance, friendship, as well as criticism. Some groups also manage to be "tough" following the idea that tough love is definitely a form of love—those are the best ones.

In a workshop, there's an exchange which comes of trust. You participate both as reader and as writer. Even the leader should come as close as possible to being an equal partner in the exchange. Everyone has something to learn—and to teach.

Here are some of my rules. First of all, resist everything (at least privately). The piece is yours. Own it. When a suggestion seems so good it breaks down that resistance, then leap on it. It's what you wished you'd thought of but didn't. Second, steal.

Sometimes we are hesitant to take someone else's ideas, as though that were "cheating." Those ideas arose from the reading of your piece, probably were generated by something in the piece that you put there, so accept the advice and go on from there. Third, remember that you are your own best teacher. By articulating something about someone else's work, you'll be forming an aesthetic which will inform your *own* work. You do yourself the best service when you pay close attention to the work of others.

Finally, I do believe that you can go to a workshop too soon, before you've become sure of yourself as a writer. If that happens, I think they can destroy confidence just as much as they build it. In those instances, the leader is crucial, and sometimes workshop leaders are more interested in being brilliant than in being astute. As I said, there are dangers. And we ought to remember that Faulkner, Joyce, Flaubert, et. al. did not have "workshops" and would probably have laughed at the idea. At their best, they might provide a two- or three-year shortcut in your own writing development—and some lasting friendships.

Lola Haskins On Workshops

Workshops can be watering cans or species-specific pesticides. In the latter case, if you happen to be the right sort of plant, the competition withers and you thrive. In the former, everyone grows. What I'd look for in a workshop, if there's a mentor involved, is diversity of output. If the work coming out seems pretty much the same kind of thing, then I'd be suspicious. I'd figure the person running the group was, consciously or not, imposing his or her viewpoint on the group. If there's no mentor involved, then I'd look for two things—a we're-in-this-together spirit, and, again, diversity, but diversity within reason. Advice from a rabid Ashberry fan might not be much use to someone who wanted to write like Jared Carter or Andrea Budy.

So, assuming the right workshop, then the question arises as to how far you should let it shape your work. Well, for me the rule of thumb is the rule of three. If three people whose opinion I respect make the same comment, then I feel I need to take it seriously, maybe not do what they suggest but at least acknowledge that there's something wrong with that part of the poem and try to fix it. Actually, often I come up with a solution which isn't anything anyone suggested but just the result of my having taken a closer look. Which wouldn't have happened if it hadn't been for the group.

Andrea Hollander Budy On Writing To Please

I wrote poems without taking any classes in poetry writing for five years; then I participated in a single semester-long poetry workshop with the late Richard Hugo. What I learned from that experience was (1) that in my five years previous to the workshop experience, I had already developed good work habits (i.e., I had taught myself how to revise), and (2) that it was important to continue to develop my work before I ever thought about having any of it published.

I learned the latter through an unusual experience: Praise from Richard Hugo led to atrophy in me: for weeks after he praised my initial poems, I could not write. How did this come about? I'm not sure I know, exactly. Except that I liked the praise so much that my motivation for writing was temporarily altered. In other words, because I received high praise from Richard Hugo about the first poems I brought to the workshop, I had difficulty returning to my writing desk without bringing into my room the elation of that praise. Because of it, I wanted (for the first time) to write poems that *the teacher* would like rather than devoting myself to work that came from only me. I was willing, suddenly, to take fewer risks, to want only to imitate my own successful poems (so that I would have more praise).

Thus, I learned that it was important—at least for me—to

write without the burden of knowing that I would be showing it to a specific someone else. For this and other reasons, I did not send work out to magazines and journals for another five years—ten years altogether since my poetry career began. I simply wanted to *write* more than I wanted to *have written*. It was an important lesson: I had to know when I sent my first poems out to the editors of magazines that *even if the poems were accepted*, such acceptance would not stop me from writing new poems.

Recommended Assignments

Beginning Level
Attend a writing conference in your area or enroll in a community workshop. Keep a journal after each session session and later analyze whether your workshop experience helped improve the level of your writing and critiquing skills.

Intermediate Level
Enroll in or audit an academic workshop in a nearby college. Keep a journal after each session and record whether this kind of workshop experience improved your writing and critiquing skills. Compare your journal entries with the ones you made in the previous assignment, if appropriate.

Advanced Level
Organize a private workshop and use your experiences in other workshops to design one that suits your style and/or aesthetics or that motivates you via support of friends.

Chapter Two

Doing Poetry Readings

*There's something heroic about poetry reading mavins; they
endure while lesser souls around them succumb to coma*

—Colette Inez

The Role Of Readings

POETS WORK ALONE. At best they know local poets from work-
shops and network with others by mail or telephone. Typically,
family and friends read what a poet writes and may over- or
underreact to verse because they know or *think* that they know
the author in question. Eventually, a poet has to guess at the
quality of his or her work by the number of poems published or
the number of rejections amassed, and both barometers are
unreliable; perhaps poems were accepted because the verse was
trendy or rejected because the verse was too experimental or
far-sighted for the audience. Or bad. Or great. Or just plain
mediocre because the editor was.

One way to find out is to do a reading. Poets tend to think
about readings the way they think about acceptance slips:

another notch on the resumé or vita. Something to puff the ego. Something to justify all that time spent laboring at your desk. But a reading, actually, is an opportunity to test your work with strangers and ascertain their response. Were they visibly moved? Bored? Cool to some poems and warm to others? Why?

Readings tell you more about your work than an editor or teacher ever could in a workshop. To make this point to four aspiring poets in one of my workshops, I scheduled an unusual reading for them. The event was sponsored by the Advertising Club in the Journalism Department of a major university and attended by students who expressed no interest in poetry. (They were given extra credit to attend.) Each student also was given a survey to rate the work of the various poets and to make general comments. Critiques were encouraged.

The poets read their best verse, and the audience loved it. (Only five out of eighty disliked the reading.) However, most of the listerners praised three of the four readers that night. The fourth reader wasn't criticized, but overlooked, and later he concluded that his poems did not connect with the audience. Thereafter he took readings and reader-response more seriously, entered a creative writing program, and eventually published his work in magazines (including *Poetry*). In sum, his reading that night was not successful but led, at least in part, to his ultimate success as a poet.

Readings can have that power. That's why some poets avoid them, unwilling to be tainted by the tastes of the typical listener. They want their creativity to be free of judgment and compose, essentially, for themselves. They feel that poets who write with an audience in mind are being untrue to their muses. If you feel this way, fine. But remember that art is meant to be appreciated and that craft is part of the art-making process, and if you shun poetry readings, you eliminate an important tool of craft: your relationship with the listener. Doing readings to puff egos is one thing. Doing them to ascertain response is quite another. For instance, if you consider yourself an experimental writer on the cutting edge of incomprehensibility and do a reading at the local diner, and everyone at the counter relates to your work and understands your metaphors and symbols, well, alas—this also tells you something!

Finally, people who attend poetry readings can be important in your career as a writer. Usually you will meet other poets, writers, editors, librarians, artists, musicians, and ordinary interesting folks who may influence or inspire you and later even buy your books when you publish them. This, of course, is part of the networking process. In fact, many of the poets who will share their verse and advice with you in this book—including three writers featured in this chapter—became my business associates because I attended their readings or they attended mine.

Now that we have established the role of readings, let's see how you can arrange one.

Poetry Slams

The easiest way to test the waters—some will say to plunge right into them!—is to show up at a poetry "slam." Slams are public poetry competitions. Poets read their verse and members of the audience judge them. Winners usually get small prizes—$25, $20, $10—for first, second, and third, although sometimes the purse is higher in major U.S. cities. Slams became popular in the early 1990s at places like the Green Mill Lounge in Chicago and at the Nuyorican Poets Cafe in New York City.

In a 16 December 1991 article in *Time,* author Janice C. Simpson describes a slam as "a literary version of *The Gong Show.*" That's the best definition I know. A word of warning, however: Slams are high-powered events. The audience wants poems that can excite or move them emotionally. You may be cheered or put down, depending on the ability of your verse to connect with listeners. That means the brooding poet in the English department might be booed if he reads that obtuse meditation on existentialism in the latest edition of *Sulfur.* Conversely, the upbeat part-time waiter who scribbles a few crisp lines on the latest war in the Middle East can wow the same audience and win.

Thus, slams are ideal for poets with healthy egos who want to work on voice, clarity, and message in their verse. They are less than ideal for shy or self-doubting poets or ones who want to improve such elements of craft as theme, metaphor, and structure.

To illustrate, I'd read this poem at a slam because its voice is passionate and its message, clear:

> *I Know*
>
> Harder things to do than give your body
> Up, the golden rope of hair, the touch
> I love and lost. I cannot think of any
>
> Reason to remain the understudy:
> Bed's a stage; the role (for me) a cinch.
> I know harder acts to do. Give your body
>
> To another or a few, but not to me.
> I leave it willingly. It does not matter much
> To lose one type of love. Think of any
>
> Body, yet not mine! Let mine be free
> Of taint, entanglement. Of kiss or clutch
> Or harder things. I could give your body
>
> Up like lent, a wife, a son I never see,
> Who has my body type and blood: O, such
> Loss is easy with love. Just think of any
>
> Number of things we leave behind, a family,
> A horse, a house, a church, and do not flinch.
> So I should know the ways to give your body
> Up, my love. *But I cannot think of any.*

I wouldn't read the following poem, even though it won The Hoephner Award at *Southern Humanities Review,* because it pivots on a subtle theme—love's fragility—using delicate couplets and elevated diction:

Prognosis of the Pupa

The bloody heart has a bypass,
The broken leg has a splint,

The bloody limb has a bandage,
But broken auricles

Never mend or if so,
Take a suture

Of raw braided silk
Lovers reel on a filature

Of monarch cocoon
So the bloom time unravels

The incubating cup.
Anthers of hope also burst.

The pupae that drop
And ping the earth

May not pilgrim
The mosque of a tulip

But succumb anyhow to the heart
Unable to absorb

The healing line that haunts it.

While the poems "I Know" and "Prognosis of the Pupa" are both love lyrics, the directness of the voice in the first poem and the melody of the rhyme and repeating lines are better suited to a slam. Members of the audience would cringe at the second poem, booing such highfalutin words as "filature" and "anthers" and missing puns like "auricles/oracles" (noticed by the eye instead of the ear).

In addition to love poems, political and social-minded ones on such controversial issues as war, violence and abuse often go over powerfully at slams. The audience, fed up with the diluted or convoluted messages of mass media, yearns to hear the truth. And slammers provide it via verse. Almost every major city features slams on weekends or special nights. You don't have to live near a metropolitan area, however, to persuade the local cafe manager to host such an event. If the popularity of poetry slams is on the wane in your neighborhood, help rekindle it by tying the slam to a holiday like Halloween or an occasion like Spring Break. Tell the manager that you'll be glad to distribute fliers announcing the "theme" of the slam to attract a good crowd of poets and judges.

You might want to attend a slam or two beforehand, however, to get a feel of how readers perform their verse and how it is received by the audience. As any slammer will tell you, such variables as the atmosphere of a lounge or even the hour—early when customers are less roudy, or late when they are more so—are contributing factors. So pick your poems carefully before you step up to the mike, reading your more clever pieces earlier and your more passionate ones, later in the evening.

You don't have to slam in a bar, though. The ballroom of a ritzy hotel or the balcony of a public mall is just fine, given the right mix of people. Without a doubt, performance poetry can be a collective *and* thematic experience.

For instance, a Washington, D.C., group called The Spoken Word emphasizes the ancient African oral tradition in its presentations. Group member Joy Jones says in the June 1993 *Writer's Digest* that The Spoken Word often is in demand in February because of Black History Month. But, she adds, "I'm convinced that *any* poet or group of poets could develop a theme that would lead to a niche in the marketplace."

Jones sees another benefit, however. "At our practice sessions, and even at our performances, there are often discussions—no, *debates*—about the viewpoints and concepts expressed in the poems. Since writing is so often a solitary act, this interaction has been one of the group's greatest benefits." Interaction between poet and audience is the chief benefit of performance poetry.

How To Slate Other Types Of Readings

Local readings are the easiest to schedule. You can solicit them through various social clubs or church groups or through libraries and school districts. If you write children's poems, in particular, the library is a great resource and children a greater audience. (Believe me, you'll know after your first poem if they are excited or bored by your verse.) Or, if you want to write poems for science fiction magazines, contact nearby SF organizations or ask advisers of Science Clubs at area schools if you can read your work during one of their monthly meetings. (Most SF groups and Science Clubs welcome speakers, and members usually enjoy discussing poems and participating in critiques.)

Many book stores host readings, especially for local writers. If your book store doesn't, visit with the manager and state your case: readings bring in new customers. Or read the "Arts and Entertainment" page of your newspaper to get a feel for the type of events in your locale. You will be surprised at the number of offerings in the typical community or near-by city. In my own small town this week, for example, more than a dozen events are slated at local cafes, museums, and college departments. In the nearest city, more than one hundred events are scheduled. Moreover, area newspapers publish calendars of art-related events and provide addresses and telephone numbers of sponsors. Make contact. Then make a pitch.

Finally, almost every town has a cable company and each franchise a public access channel. Radio stations have to serve the public interest if they want to utilize the public airwaves. Both solicit programming ideas on a regular basis. Visit with station managers and see if you can arrange to tape a cassette or make a video for broadcast. (While broadcast readings won't provide you with an immediate response to your work, listeners or viewers eventually will let you know what they think; moreover, you will have a "demonstration" tape to show other sponsors when soliciting new readings.)

Arranging readings at English departments—the most common sponsor of such events—can be difficult. Unless you are publishing regularly in literary journals and have a book-length collection in print, you won't be invited to read at a college. On the other hand, many universities attract large crowds for literary events by hosting "open mikes" before or after readings by well-known poets. An "open mike" session usually is a five-minute presentation of one to three poems by select members of the audience. Usually, these poets are chosen after signing a sheet posted at the reading. Rules vary. So check with English Department representatives to see whether their readings include "open mike" sessions or, if not, whether they would be willing to sponsor them. If possible, take advantage of the opportunity. The "open mike" is a chance for you to read your work to a large audience and to get frank opinions from professors and poets. As you can see, there is no end to the possibilities of arranging a reading in your area. Once you get one, however, you have to promote it to ensure good attendance.

How To Publicize Your Reading

Promoting a reading takes initiative and drive. After you have arranged a place and time to read, design a flier announcing the event. On a good sheet of bond paper, type the time and place in a prominent spot in capital letters and then include a few sentences about you and/or poems that you plan to read. If you have a computer, print the time and place of your reading in a larger font or headline style. If you want, glue a small photograph (or mugshot) of you on the original page for visual appeal. Above all, resist the urge to fill the flier with needless information. The more white space, the easier the flier will be to read.

Here's a typical flier:

POETRY READING
SUNDAY, AUGUST 23, AT 3 P.M.
IN THE FRONT ROOM OF BAKER CENTER
OHIO UNIVERSITY

JANE SMITH, local poet,
will read from her new
work about the environment.
She has published verse
in such magazines as
*Prairie Schooner, Beloit,
Poets On:,* and *Ascent.*

Picture of
Jane Smith

Smith's reading is part of The Front Room's annual
series of poetry and fiction presentations, co-sponsored
by the Student Senate and English Department. Before
Smith's reading, there will be an "open mike" session
for local poets to read one or two samples of their work.
Sign-up sheet will be posted in the lobby at 2:30 P.M.

Refreshments will be provided following the reading.

After you have designed a similar flier, photocopy it on colored paper (pink or yellow). Avoid darker colors like red and blue because the printed information will be harder to read. Then post the fliers in strategic places: cafes, bookshops, malls, schools, community bulletin boards. (Always ask permission when posting fliers and do not staple them to power poles or trees or otherwise litter the outdoors.) Finally, even though your fliers should contain the day *and* the date, post them one week before the event to avoid confusion about what *day* the reading is slated. For instance, you would post the above flier about Jane Smith's Sunday reading no earlier than *Monday,* August 17. If you posted the flier earlier, some people would mistake "Sunday" for August 16.

Also be sure to contact the Arts and Entertainment editor one week before the reading so that he or she can list the event in the community calendar. Do the same with the radio and cable stations. Some weekly newspapers and shopper tabloids offer free space in the classifieds for personal annoucements; again, list the reading. Church or club bulletins and library newsletters also provide such space.

You may want to write a short news release in the concise style of your community newspaper or broadcast station. Again, send it one week before the event to the managing editor of the newspaper or general manager of the station. Here's a sample release about Jane Smith's reading at The Front Room:

∽

FOR IMMEDIATE RELEASE   Contact: Jane Smith
                                         0000 Main Street
                                         Athens, OH 45701
                                         (614) 555-3737

ATHENS—Local poet Jane Smith will read from her poems about the environment on Sunday, August 23, at 3 p.m. in the Front Room of Baker Center at Ohio University.

Smith's poems deal with the effects of global warming and the politics of ecology. Smith, a science teacher at the Middle School, has published more than 40 poems in literary magazines, including *Prairie Schooner, Beloit, Poets On:,* and *Ascent.*

As a special feature, an "open mike" session will precede Smith's reading. Local poets are invited to share one or two of their verses. A sign-up sheet with more information about the open session will be posted in the lobby of the Baker Center two hours before the event.

The reading, co-sponsored by the Student Senate and English Department at OU, is the fifth this year in the annual series of poetry and fiction presentations.

Following Smith's reading, the Student Senate will host a reception. Refreshments will be provided.

The reading and reception are free to the public.

~

(Editors: Smith is available for interviews during the hours of 9-5 p.m. daily and all day Saturday.)

Finally, get out the word to family and friends. Mail or deliver copies of your flier. Always write something personal on the flier or include a letter because these are the people who have supported you as a poet. You can even let friends and acquaintances know about your reading by recording a short announcement on your telephone answering machine: "I'm unable to answer the phone right now, but if you leave your name and number, I'll call you back as soon as I can. By the way, I hope to see you on Sunday at 3 p.m. in the Front Room of Baker Center when I will be doing a reading. Please come. I'll need your support!"

After you have promoted the event, you should concentrate on perfecting your performance.

How To Prepare For A Reading

Assemble a selection of poems that are related thematically or that tell or imply a story when read in sequence. The best readings feature poems that probe a topic or relate an incident or series of incidents based on your core beliefs. You want to convey your deepest convictions. If you are working on new poems and want to get a feel for their effect on an audience, slip a few of these into the mix so that you can measure response when these are juxtaposed to your most accomplished verse. Usually you won't have to solicit people's critiques—they'll gladly provide them at the reception following the reading. (If not, ask.)

If you are too shy to solicit critiques, you might ask a friend to help you. For example, when I do a reading, I telephone an acquaintance beforehand who plans to attend. I ask if she would be willing to serve as my official critic and give me a frank assessment of how my poems sounded when read aloud. Afterward, I quiz her: "Were you confused by any lines or images? Did you have a favorite or a least favorite poem? Which poems seemed to go over best (worst) with the audience?" Of course, your questions will differ, depending on what you want to measure at the reading.

If you have never done a reading before, it is a good idea to tape-record yourself so that you can hear your voice. Most beginning readers recite poems too quickly, so make a conscious effort to slow down the cadence to allow listeners to appreciate each hard-earned line of your verse. At first, the slow cadence will sound unnatural to you, but you will reap the benefits soon enough. Commit to the work. I gave this advice to Grace Rutledge, a southern California poet, and soon after she gave a reading and wrote me: "I did not read too fast. In fact, I read the few poems and excerpts from my short stories as if they *deserve* to be read—I committed to the material. My reward was that people of all ages and backgrounds came up to see where I'd be reading next, or where they could get my book."

Award-winning writer Nancy Kress, whom I heard read at a literary conference in New York, relates: "My biggest problem when I first began to read was that I inevitably read too fast, partly from nervousness and partly because I talk fast anyway. So for the first few years I gave public readings, I would ask a friend to sit in the front row and pull on his/her ear if I was going too fast, as a signal to slow down. This worked fairly well until a friend kept pulling and pulling and I kept slowing and slowing, ultimately to what sounded to me like HAL winding down in *2001*. It turned out she had forgotten all about her trust and was playing with her earring."

Kress says that she prepares for a reading by scanning her material over the night or afternoon before the event to make sure that she can pronounce everything. This is something many novice poets overlook. Often they are surprised that they use words that they can spell . . . but cannot pronounce. Or words that look peachy on the page but tie the tongue in knots when said aloud. Kress's advice eliminates that concern.

Another well-known writer, poet and novelist Karen Joy Fowler, takes a light-hearted approach when she reads. She doesn't prepare much in advance for readings other than selecting her material and making a few notations on a scrap of paper. "To do more would make me nervous," she says. "What I do is pretend that I am not giving a reading. I pretend so successfully that I rarely am nervous at all. This works quite well up until the very moment when I have to rise from wherever I am seated and go stand in front of an audience. Then I realize I'm about to give a reading. And it is always such a surprise."

Fowler often begins her readings by reciting someone else's work—"a poem or two," she says. "This eases me into the reading and gets me past the point at which I am most nervous. There is always the risk that one's own work pales by comparison, of course, but I can't see that as a good reason not to read some piece that I really love."

Fowler also jots down a few sentences to introduce each poem to the audience. Typically, poets often add a personal touch by describing how they came to write a specific piece or what, exactly, moved them to write about a certain incident. (In any case, the introduction should be no more than a few sentences; long intros to poems detract from the poetry and often bore or embarrass the audience, spoiling the mood.) Consider the impact of a poet saying—"I wrote this piece about holes in the ozone because I realized that even the earth is mortal"—as opposed to:

> "I don't believe in this ozone nonsense, but many editors do, so I thought I'd write an environmental poem and get published."

Try as you may, eventually you will say something that you regret when you wing it at the podium. If so, forget it as soon as possible and get on with the reading. When things go wrong, take yourself lightly (along with a lighter approach). Listen to how Karen Joy Fowler deals with this concern: "As I have given more and more readings, I find myself repeating the same stories, the same explanations. My energy level drops accordingly. So I force myself to go in alternate directions. I try to say at least one ill-considered thing that I will deeply regret at each reading. This is easy to accomplish and keeps my energy level high."

Let's end with some tips.

Final Word On Readings

If you have never done a reading before, you need to know:

1. *Length of presentation.* Typically, a one-person reading averages between 40 minutes and one hour. A 30-minute reading lapses too quickly for listeners who have changed their routines or based their plans for an evening or afternoon around your event. On the other hand, readings approaching one hour or more often exhaust the listeners—the ear can only take so much—and patience wears thin. The ideal reading should conclude at about 45 minutes, leaving about 15 for the reception.

To ascertain how long your reading will take, assemble your poems according to theme or story and then read them aloud as you would at the event, timing yourself. Then add or delete poems as necessary.

2. *Length of dual readings.* Often you will share the stage with another poet or writer. Typically, each of you will be asked to present a 20- to 30-minute reading. If you agree to go first, the audience will still be fresh at 20 to 30 minutes and the impulse will be to read an additional 10 minutes or so. Don't do it. It's unfair to the second reader who will lose the audience after an hour. If, however, someone reads before you do and continues reading beyond his or her allocated time, don't interrupt or otherwise signal your discontent. Accept the situation. If you become visibly angry or upset, you will be in no mood to face the public and might even read your work in an irritated voice.

Sooner or later the first poet will look at his or her watch. Meanwhile, look over your selected poems and delete as many as you think will be necessary to complete the reading on time. Eliminate introductions to poems or anecdotes and recite as many poems as possible before the hour ends. Occasionally this will mean reading as few as three poems. Do so and end the session on an upbeat note, thanking the audience for attending. Remember your quarrel is with the first poet and that organizers of the event will understand why you read so briefly. (If not, tell them.) They will appreciate your professionalism and probably invite you to do another reading.

3. *Setting for the reading.* I have read poems in newsrooms of major newspapers and on the stairwells of Colonial mansions. It helps to know beforehand what the setting will be. If you show up for a reading thinking that you will be at the podium in an auditorium and learn at the last minute that you'll be reading on a stool in the lobby of a hotel, you may feel unsettled and that can affect your attitude. There also can be technical concerns. If your reading is outdoors, be sure someone has set up a microphone.

In general, it's a good idea to arrive 15 minutes early at the site and to become familiar with the surroundings.

4. *Dress code for readings.* There is none. Wear clothes that make you feel comfortable. If you feel comfortable in a suit or formal gown, wear or rent one. If you feel comfortable in T-shirt and jeans, put them on. You may want to avoid dressing up like Hollywood's version of a poet with ascot or headband because it might make you seem pretentious and artificial. But if you feel comfortable with an ascot or a headband, don one or both of them.

Your poetry should make a statement, not your fashion sense.

Guidebook

Colette Inez On Readings

Perhaps as a resident of both sides of the podium, I qualify to pass along a few tips which for me—during 400 or more stage appearances over the last twenty years—have served, at least, to keep audiences awake, the first and possibly the greatest challenge for the reader-performer.

1. Forget the business about the immortal integrity of the written word, the fallback positions of some readers who drone on with bottomless epics better reserved for the eye, not the ear. Reading poetry is part show biz and demands pacing, a sense of delivery, pause and incidental patter.

2. Mix and match. Combine solemnity with wit, longer poems with epigrammatic quickies you may stock in your repertoire. Reserve sharp poems of tested power for curtain raisers and closers.

3. Try yourself on you. Dry run your style on a tape recorder and tune in for flaws with an impartial ear. Does the delivery do the poem justice? Would you as a listener give yourself a sigh or an ovation?

4. A short introduction should precede your poems. Be serious, funny, preposterous but hone down those nifty anecdotes lest what follows is a letdown.

5. Histrionics are out. Elocution, trills, oratory, turn me off. I begin to suspect that behind all that chromium is a lot of defective metal. At the opposite pole, and just as rankling, is the flat, toneless reading that suggests the poet is really an android.

6. Don't apologize for missteps. If you skip a line, stumble over a word, start again or sail on.

7. If a shared reading permits, ask for the final berth. You'll get a chance to electrify an audience narcotized by the first reader who failed to read these counsels.

Note: For more tips by Ms. Inez, see her contributions in *Poets on Stage* (Release Press, 1978), from which the advice above has been updated and adapted.

Jim Barnes On Readings

Who in the name of holy hell or heaven has any more right to present your work than you do? You hope your voice is Dylanesque or Burtonic. But even though you may butcher the verbs and skin the nouns, you've sunk your meat hook into the beast and pulled it up for full display. And be grateful for the audience, those few extraordinary people who drift out of the crowd and down into the hollow to hear the echoes of your songs.

Susan Ludvigson On Readings

It's always been my theory that an audience—even a sophisticated poetry audience, knowledgeable and accustomed to hearing poems read aloud—can only sustain concentration for a relatively brief period. If a single poet is reading, I assume 40-60 minutes is the maximum attention span; if more than one poet is reading, so that the voices change, maybe the audience will still be attentive up to 1 1/2 hrs. Possibly if one is about twenty years old, the attention span is longer, I can't remember! Unfortunately, open mike readings, in my experience, tend to go on for hours. Hearing wonderful poems by wonderful poets can be sublime; hearing too many poems, some of which, pretty much by definition, are not likely to be wonderful, can be excruciating.

Fred Chappell On Slams

My son Heath is drummer for many slams at the Green Mill in Chicago and has promised to send tapes but hasn't yet done so. One is always, upon hearing news of fashions of these sorts, rather glad that poetry is gathering some attention. The slams are hard evidence that people do not hate poetry—as most teachers of the stuff tell us continually. People like it, they will drive across town to hear it and say it, they are willing to be teased and maybe embarrassed and possibly humiliated in order to pursue it in its livliest and, I'd suspect, sometimes its rawest forms. I will repeat my long cherished belief that poetry is a physiognomic necessity for the human organism. Only neighborhood baseball and softball team members are willing to put as much on the line as poetry slammers.

And there is no way these activists are fooling themselves that what they say and hear is the greatest poetry ever conceived or uttered. They know exactly where it stands in relation to Milton, Eliot, Tennyson, and Pope. But they understand too that the pleasures of poetry take multifoliate shapes and that the poetry of spontaneity can offer the same kind of enjoyment that an evening of jazz can. It offers too the same fleeting disappointments, of course—but without those there *is* no delight of the other kind.

Recommended Assignments

Beginning Level

1. Attend as many readings as possible and afterward make some notes in your journal. How long did the session last? Was it a single or dual reading? Slam? Open mike? How did the poet begin and end the presentation? Did he or she introduce poems with anecdotes? How did the audience respond? Record anything else of interest that happens during a reading, analyze your notes, and then add what you liked or disliked about the event.

2. If you think you are ready to do a public reading, try an open mike or slam because they require only a few poems. Afterward, assess your performance in your journal.

Intermediate Level

Using methods explained in this chapter, arrange a reading of your poems. Do the promotion. Prepare. Follow tips. Refer to those pages in your journal in which you discussed the previous assignment, if appropriate. Review those entries. Now plan an ideal reading. At the reception, ask questions about individual poems and determine which ones moved or confused the audience. Afterward, in your journal, write about your first reading (arranging, promoting, preparing, and performing) and describe what went right and what could have gone better.

Advanced Level

Arrange another reading using methods described in this chapter. Read your journal containing entries based on exercises from the Beginning and Intermediate Levels. Promote the reading. Prepare. Follow tips. At the reception, ask members of the audience for critiques. Afterward, evaluate all phases of your reading again and make more recommendations to improve your performance.

Chapter Three

Entering Contests

Why do I and others persist year after year in entering selected contests? Because it's still well worth the effort, not necessarily because you're going to enjoy instant fame but because the greatest reward is the fact that you work and re-work your poems in preparation for the event. You push yourself to the limit and spend the necessary time a finished work demands. You make damned sure your work is as good as it can possibly be. Then, after enclosing the MS, the check, the SASE and mailing it, you throw salt to the devil, spit three times, and pray

—Ruth Daigon

Types Of Contests

CONTESTS REMAIN ONE of the best paths to launch a writing career. In the 1980s, when I was just starting out as a poet, I won or placed in two dozen contests and have claimed prizes as modest as parchment, as odd as Hummels and bowls, and as generous as $1,000. In fact, I garnered my first honorable mention in the 1980 *Writer's Digest* competition and would go on to place in the top 100 five more times. In 1993, I judged the contest for the first time. The *WD* competition falls in the category of contests by writing magazines, one of the most trustworthy types of sponsors. If you win one of these, you know that your entry has a modicum of merit because the reputation and impartiality of the magazine are at stake. Prizes usually are generous, and the prestige factor is high.

Other major sponsors include:

1. *Literary contests.* Usually these are sponsored by publications at colleges and universities and have a higher prestige factor than all other types of contests. Prize money can range from a few dollars to hundreds of dollars. If you win or place in one, you should list it in cover letters when you market poems and in contributor's notes when you publish them.

2. *Small-press contests.* These are sponsored by editors who own publications with small circulations. The prestige factor varies according to the reputation of the magazine in question. Prize money can range from a few dollars to hundreds of dollars. If you win or place in one, you should list it in cover letters and contributor's notes.

3. *Group contests.* These are sponsored by writing federations and poetry societies. The prestige factor varies because such groups usually host dozens of contests each year to keep members active and competitive. Prize money usually is small at the local or state level, but high at the national level. If you win state or national honors, you should list these in cover letters and contributor's notes.

4. *Private contests.* These are not associated with magazines and are sponsored by institutions, foundations, and corporations. Some are considered prestigious, and some not. Some will enhance your reputation, and some won't. Prize money can range from a few dollars to thousands of dollars. You should list your awards in cover letters or contributor's notes, or should keep them secret, depending on the reputation of the specific contest.

As you can see, all contests are not equal. But if you win a major one like the *Writer's Digest* competition, your name will be publicized and that can lead to more contacts and greater acclaim. Contests also provide poets with a little pocket money and a lot of encouragement. Conversely, you should feel no remorse if you fail to place in a contest because, typically, it only means that on one particular day, a judge with particular tastes, decided that someone else's work appealed to him or her more than yours. Remember, it's nice to win a contest, but it's so much easier to lose one, especially when you compete with hundreds of poets.

The Typical Contest

Let's focus on the *Writer's Digest* poetry contest because it is representative and based on merit considerations. (Indeed, early in their careers, such noted poets as Raymond Carver and Carolyn Forché placed in the top 100.) As such, observations about this particular contest apply to all bonafide ones. Conducted for decades as part of the magazine's annual writing competition, it features:

- Entry blank with rules.
- Small fees to accompany entries.
- Deadline for entries.
- Competition with hundreds of poets.
- Impartial judges whose decisions are final.

When I was just starting out as a writer, one of my life-goals was to place in the annual competition. Fifteen years later I did with a poem that came in 14th place. I would enter each year thereafter and would place 50th, 8th, 52nd, no show, 3rd, and 10th. In time I realized that to win the *WD* contest—or any contest, for that matter—you need three ingredients:

1. *Inspiration.* The poetry of previous winners should set a standard that inspires you to enter the contest.

2. *Persistence.* Once you decide to enter a contest, you should

keep entering each year until you win or are satisfied that you tried your best to win.

3. *Information.* If you have never entered a contest before, it helps to know others who have and who can provide some tips.

Consequently, I asked four poets who have won previous *WD* competitions to share their works to inspire you, their anecdotes about contests to help you persist, and their tips about contests to give you an edge. Then I'll give you an idea of how judging is done behind the scenes. We'll begin with Stephen Corey, associate editor of *The Georgia Review.* Corey won the 1981 *WD* poetry competition with this inspiring entry:

Hearing With My Son

> *Our studies show that the autistic*
> *child apparently has a random relationship*
> *with sounds, linking them with whatever*
> *object holds his attention at the moment.*

Crouched by his chair, my son hears
my complaint from the wine glass,
my praise from his own shoe.
When I read him books, I speak
through their pictures, or the wall.

Despite my love, I say less and less—
even if he heard me in the trees
or the sunset, he would not listen.

Perhaps, somewhere on the soft and hot
savannahs of Kenya, a newborn gazelle
speaks with the voice of my son.

He throws his cup across the room.
His hand explodes with the crash.

Of all the poems that Corey has written and published since, in the best journals and magazines, this remains one of my favorites. In essence, the narrator throws his voice—the sound on the page—through a series of objects and images associated with childhood. The lyric takes on a surreal tone, precisely one we need to experience the son's condition. Finally, in the last two lines, the reader understands autism.

Corey says, "As I look back a dozen years to the writing of 'Hearing With My Son,' I believe that whatever success and staying power the poem may have are the result of my having managed to focus—tenderly but relentlessly—on the father's emotional state."

He also notes that in composing the poem, he tried to avoid "simplistic" resolutions and "self-pity."

Jim Hall, the judge who chose Corey's poem that year, said he did so because the images don't call attention to themselves. "There is control and coherency in this poem. And there's something that beginning poets often think is their enemy: logic. The logic of this poem is the logic of a normal person facing a profoundly illogical world."

Corey puts it another way: "The mind will jabber on with its 'logic' and 'reason,' but the heart never says an unessential word."

I like his explanation better. To win the *WD* competition, or any contest based on merit, each word of your entry has to count. Competition is always keen. There are other considerations, too. To familiarize you with them, let's focus on the histories and entires of award-winning poets Marion Brimm Rewey, Judi K. Beach, and R. Nikolas Macioci.

Rewey entered the *WD* competition repeatedly, with these results: 1979 (8th Place), 1980 (2nd Place), 1982 (38th Place), 1987 (17th Place), 1988 (46th Place), 1989 (4th Place), and, finally, the Grand Prize. "The *Writer's Digest* win was the peak," she says, noting that she also won the grand prize from the National Federation of State Poetry Societies and dozens of prizes from other contests.

Rewey notes that she began entering the *WD* contest "as a discipline." First, the 16-line limit was a challenge because she tends to write longer poems. Second, she had researched the market and knew that the *WD* competition had a reputation for impartiality and merit, unlike a few others "in this day of 'pay to be published' contests as ego boosters," she says. Third, she had faith in herself and her work. Here is her Grand Prize-winning poem:

On Fading To Invisible

It takes longer now to find her hiding place.

Each year she digs in deeper, turns all mirrors to the wall,
averts her eyes in public places to blunt indifferent looks from
    strangers.

Her supple grace quite past,
she exists on pretty lies she tells herself
such as: beauty is within, it shines through eyes,
and knows, in bleakness of night-wakes, facade is all.

Without the proper one she disappears,
erased by stares that blindly skim past pain.

Each day she sketches in lost parts.
Line by line she paints new lies,
bone by bone puffs up that day's esteem.
This done, she peeks around her shrouded window,
creeps out in morning sun,

and tries and tries
but cannot seem to cast the faintest shadow.

Like Stephen Corey's poem, Rewey's lyric sets a high standard. The narrator starts with a powerful first line; uses free verse to augment her wide-ranging, plaintive, and introspective voice; and depicts theme via images—the slow disappearance of selfhood—ending with a scene that implies an epiphany.

The same attention to craft is found in the winning entires of Judi K. Beach and R. Nikolas Macioci. Beach entered the

WD competition once in 1989 and placed second. Then, years later, she entered again and won with this short narrativ...

After The Argument

She turns from his rumpled breathing,
from his warm hand sleeping on her thigh.
She pushes blankets like a woolen boundary
between them. The shadow arms of sassafras stretch
across the wall. He snuffles and shifts
to his side, carrying the covers with him.
The streetlight paves her way to the hall.
In the cool pre-dawn of the kitchen,
she leans against the sill staring
into the slow light which opens on the garden
and thinks how the breaths of the trees
this morning match his in the middle of night.
The kettle sings. Her blackberry tea,
the color of a fresh bruise. Sleep
falls from her like an opened robe.

You can see how this entry caught the eye of Diane Wakoski, the judge that year. The poem contains a dramatic title that also sets the tone of the narrative to follow. The author chooses a moment of narration that doesn't allow for much comment but that depicts action, adding to the tension. Finally, she implies the outcome of the argument by using sensory images in the final three lines, the last of which is the most powerful in the poem.

R. Nikolas Macioci entered the annual contest seven times before placing second in the 1991 competition with this nature lyric:

Half Spring

A single, blinding, instantaneous blaze
catches the earth, slowly angles it up
out of the rough. Suddenly this is the best

light, twig-filling light when sky has language
and ceramic clouds shine warmth like best words.
Their winter fading, juncos survive.
Behind them, green limbs rise in velvet.
This is the time when gravity reverses
itself, climbs neglected trellises, swells
woods to solid darkness. This is the smooth hold
returning, repairing, filling hours
with hunger for the earth, for the deep flesh
of new desire. These are days that flower
behind our backs, turn yellow-white
while our hands sort garden seeds, plant
asters, bluebells, and passion flowers.

Once more, Macioci's poem has the earmarks of a prize-winner: a powerful first line, gorgeous diction, well-crafted lines, a lone stanza that sustains the fragile moment in the garden, images that depict a peak experience in nature, and, finally, an alluring last line.

To win contests, you have to compose poems that can stand alongside those of Marion Brimm Rewey, Judi K. Beach, and R. Nikolas Macioci. To do so, they say, you have to pay attention to craft because judges always look for it in entires. Moreover, they maintain, that while there is no secret formula to win poetry competitions, you *can* gain an edge by knowing some tips. Marion Brimm Rewey says:

- Tap your heritage for poems . . . but also embellish, too. "I confess I am a myth-maker, drawing on my Southern background and shamelessly mixing truth with fiction."

- Aim for emotional intensity. "You want those who read the poem to enter into it and experience the feeling."

- Be clear and concise. "I am not a fan of obscure poetry. Don't write it, don't like it. And so-called intellectual poems leave me cold."

- Emphasize rhythm and sound. "I've learned to let slant rhymes fall where they may. I hear words as music and I like to make them harmonize."

Judi K. Beach says:

- Pay attention to language. "You should rewrite, rethink, reconsider every word, always looking for the freshest way to say something, the boldest language, the correct word in meaning, sound and syntax."

- Send only your most accomplished work. "Many writers submit their work too soon. They settle for the ordinary instead of stretching for uniqueness."

- Read contemporary poets. "When I conduct a workshop, I always ask the participants how many books of poetry they have purchased in the last month. The response is deplorably low. Out of 60 or so people, an average of 4 have bought poetry in the last year, and most of those purchases were of classical poetry. Then I ask, 'How do you know what current poetry is about and who do you think will buy *your* poetry?'"

R. Nikolas Macioci says:

- Set aside time to write. "I try to spend a minimum two hours a day writing. It is typical for me to work on my writing for twelve hours at a sitting during the weekend or summer when I am not teaching."

- Subscribe to literary magazines. "I am an avid reader, but I no longer take time to enjoy very much fiction, for I spend my reading time trying to keep up with many poetry magazines. I follow with interest the careers of many other contemporary poets."

- Be professional when submitting work. "Every time I have entered a contest, I am conscientious about following guidelines. Furthermore, I think that it is important to send a clearly typed copy of your poem on clean paper. Since I will not be standing beside the judge to represent my work, I want my poem to look as good as it can."

Finally, all three poets confide that there is one more variable when it comes to winning poetry contests: luck.

"We all know talent is not enough. Luck is 90% of winning," says Marion Brimm Rewey.

Crafting (poems) is the control," says Judi K. Beach, "and luck is the variable."

R. Nikolas Macioci muses, "Sometimes I say I have just been lucky, but my brother corrects me by saying that I have made my own luck."

Let's see how you can enhance yours by discovering what goes on behind the scenes.

Judging Contests

I've judged dozens of poetry contests, including the *Writer's Digest* one. The process is both routine and agonizing:

1. *Initial Screening.* This is the routine part. The judge (or preliminary reader) simply scans each entry to make sure that it adheres to basic requirements like line length and typing format. At this point, obvious amateur attempts—poems fraught with misspellings, poor or impossible diction, wrenched rhyme—are eliminated after the judge reads a line or two.

You can complain that you sent in your fee and deserve a full reading, but the judge knows how difficult it is going to be to win the competition. One major flaw, and you're out. (That's why following contest rules and the advice of winning poets in the previous section are essential if you want to get past this point.)

Typically, if 1000 poems were entered in the competition, almost half (about 450, say) are rejected at this juncture—a sad commentary on the quality of submissions.

2. *Second Round Screening.* Now poems without major flaws are read in their entirety. Typically the judge will put them into three categories: ("No," "Maybe," "Yes") or ("Bad," "Okay," "Good") or ("Eliminated," "Still in the Running," "Possible Finalist.") In any case, the "No"/"Bad"/"Eliminated" pile of poems is rejected. Usually this represents about 350 out of the 550 remaining poems.

3. *Third Round Screening.* The focus turns to the "Maybe"/ "Okay"/"Still in the Running" category. These poems are read closely for any flaw and eliminated immediately when one is

Poet's Guide

found. The idea is to reject but also to make sure that no worthy poem is eliminated because the judge grew too tired or impatient in the second round of reading. Typically, if 100 poems are in this batch, fewer than 10 make it to the "Possible Finalist" category.

4. *Finalist Screening.* At this point the remaining category of poems usually numbers about 105-125, depending on how many made it past the third round screening. Again, the focus is on rejection, only this time, elimination becomes more difficult for the judge. The poems are read again and ones with the most minor flaws—rough meter, awkward diction, poor treatment of topic—are ousted from the batch.

5. *Final Round.* Now the agonizing part begins for the judge. Poems are read and re-read and put in a chronological order, from best to worst. The judge knows, however, that the first ranking of poems probably won't remain; so he or she puts the poems away for awhile and returns to them and re-reads, ranking the poems again.

This process continues until the judge is sure about the selections. In my case, when I judge the final round, I usually change my mind several times. By now I am quite familiar with the individual entries and usually discover a few tiny flaws—this poem could have used a better title, or this poem could have pushed the ending a bit more—and, alas, rank the poems one last time to meet my deadline and finalize my winner's list. Often the poem with no flaws—as opposed to the one with the most potential—rises to the top.

This is an awkward moment for the judge. Usually I am less happy for the winner—he or she will be elated upon hearing the good news—and more disappointed that the runners-up came so close but didn't clinch the competition. Now that you know what goes on behind the scenes, let's see how you can research contests to choose which ones you'll enter.

Because contests usually require fees, you owe it to yourself to research them. Otherwise you will be paying for the opportunity to be rejected. Moreover, some contests offer huge prizes but target the vanity of beginners who are asked to purchase expensive anthologies that carry little or no clout in the literary world. Here are more tips to help you gauge the prestige or vanity factor in poetry contests and to help you target your best work at specific competitions:

1. *Study the market.* If a magazine sponsors a contest, request a sample copy to determine whether you would want your work to appear therein. Literary and small-press competitions usually have a prestige factor, offering publication and modest prizes. Nonetheless, a handful of such contests are held to generate start-up funds or to increase subscriptions. Check marketing directories to see when a publication was founded. Generally, if it isn't listed, can't be located in the library, and is less than a year old with a circulation under 250, think twice about entering.

2. *Identify anthology presses.* Contests offering magnificent prizes often require the purchase of anthologies to cover costs. If your motivation is to claim a prize, by all means enter and refuse to buy the book (whose prices approach $50). In sum, these companies are banking on your desire to win contests and have your poems printed . . . no matter what the cost. Typically such presses also will try to sell you space in the anthology for your picture and biography, charging even higher fees. Some will offer to print up your poem in a fine font and put it in a frame. A few will sell you deluxe versions of your "award" certificate or even T-shirts. In sum, these contests are part of an overall marketing plan to get you to purchase products and services.

3. *Consider club contests.* Many states have writing societies that host contests in conjunction with conventions. Prizes are modest because dues are limited. Such competitions inspire writers by offering several awards in numerous categories,

increasing your chances. Some provide individual critiques by outside judges, increasing your chances in the future.

4. *Investigate sponsors.* Some organizations unaffiliated with magazines or writing societies host annual competitions because money has been deposited in a trust for such purposes. These include contests sponsored by universities, corporations, and individuals and usually are reputable, especially those with non-profit/tax-exempt status. In any case, before you enter, ask for lists of previous winners and/or biographies of judges. If you don't recognize any names or cannot locate them in such reference books as *A Directory of American Poets and Fiction Writers* (Poets & Writers, Inc.), then again, think twice before entering.

5. *Evaluate entry fees.* Many magazines charge entry fees to break even, covering such costs as judging, handling, and prizes. Some want a profit. Typical entry fees range between $1-5 per poem and $5-15 per piece of prose. Anything higher is suspect. You should get something for your money, too. Prestige counts in the making of a literary career, so you might want to pay $5 for a piece of parchment. A safe bet is to enter competitions that provide a free copy of the award issue or year's subscription.

6. *Send for guidelines.* Contests are usually advertised where writers see them, in freelance or literary publications. If the ad or promotion is small, guidelines won't be spelled out,so writers have to send for them to honor submission and eligibility requirements. (Always enclose an SASE.) If officials don't provide guidelines or publish an address for rules—including how much a writer has to pay, if anything, for a copy of the award issue—avoid it.

7. *Solicit winning entries.* Sponsors of competitions will be glad to sell you previous award issues. Or you can look them up in the library. Some officials provide booklets of winners, again for a fee. If you have decided to enter a contest, you might want to spring for the additional cost. The information contained in an award issue or booklet is invaluable. You'll get to see the type and style of the winning poem or prose. And while it is true that many contests feature different judges of varied tastes each year,

the staff typically screens entries. If you know its taste beforehand, you can usually decide which poem or piece of prose is appropriate for a given contest.

8. *Research judges.* Some contests announce final judges in advertisements or promotions. Others keep such information secret, fearing friends of the judge will enter and foul objectivity. Some judges see all entries without prior in-house screening. If judges are named, look up their work in the library to assess what styles, themes, or topics might appeal to them. Then check your inventory and make the appropriate selections.

9. *Obey all rules.* Serious contests have serious rules that must be obeyed. Otherwise, your entry will be eliminated and your fee deposited. Every contest has different rules and submission requirements. For instance, some call for you to submit 3-by-5 file cards listing individual titles and others, a separate cover sheet. Read each rule and check it off as you prepare your submission. Don't fudge. If the contest specifies word length or calls for a certain style or form, honor it. When your manuscript is ready for mailing, read each rule again for a final check.

10. *Submit elsewhere at risk.* Generally, reputable contests require that your submission be unpublished and not under consideration elsewhere. Occasionally, the latter requirement is omitted. Some contests have a reading cycle of six months to a year, so tying up a poem or prose manuscript may be costly. If you decide that you can't wait that long, submit elsewhere. Should your work be accepted by a magazine while under consideration at a competition, notify contest officials and offer to withdraw it. They will be glad to keep your entry fee and cross your name from their burgeoning list.

Let's close with a general rule: Enter contests because you have faith in your work, like the challenge, know the competition, are willing to take your chances, and are unwilling to be affected emotionally by the outcome.

Guidebook

Lucia Cordell Getsi On Poetry Contests

Poetry contests are both the destruction (of quality) and salvation (economic) of poetry in America. I've had a great deal of contest experience and have won maybe fifteen to twenty contests, regional to national, single poem to chapbook to book-length collections. I've judged and juried lots of contests, from school and university contests, to journal contests, to a major national contest annually that gives $1,000, $500, and $250 to the top three winners. I edit a poetry journal and have agonized over whether or not to start a contest, each year putting off the decision until the next year. I get phone calls at all hours at home, at the university, from all sorts of people asking me about bogus contests, especially from mothers who want to be told their child is a genius for winning a trip (that he must pay for to receive the prize) and the publication of his poem (in an anthology that he also must pay for).

Journal by journal and press by press, editors and publishers are capitulating to contests. Why? The economic facts: nobody reads poetry or really good fiction except those who either write it or aspire to write it or perhaps aspire to be known as writers of it. On the other hand, such writerly readers keep serious literature, poetry particularly, alive. There's no real place for it in New World Order, in which PC's generate torrents of words and pages every second, in which there is no silence and aloneness, the mother womb of poetry, except that wrested from the word-frothed jaws of TV and radio and telephones and fax machines and E-mail and America On-line and Mosaic's World-Wide Web. Journals and presses run contests to pay for the print runs of worthy publications.

Of course, the fact is that unless an editor is very careful, a contest will alter the journal running it. Maybe it will do this even when great care is exercised to see that it does not. The journal gets a flood of manuscripts right before deadline, and nobody submits much at any other time. The contest eventually runs the journal instead of the reverse. The quality changes, the types of poems the journal is known for change. Every journal has "regulars"—readers as well as writers. A contest will cause the death of this kind of writerly/readerly loyalty. The same kind of thing occurs when presses run contests to pay for the literature they publish: the press loses its identity immediately. Writers send manuscripts because there is an open invitation and often a new judge each year. The quality and type of literature the press publishes cannot be consistent unless various types of hanky-panky are practiced in advance of the final judge seeing the manuscripts, the most common being the elimination of all manuscripts that do not conform to the "image" the publisher wants to project. That seems to me particularly insidious. The publisher takes the entry fees of all, but eliminates out of hand all the entries that do not conform to the genre standard or political standard or whatever standard the publisher wants to protect. It is a kind of false advertising.

The contests that do not cause changes in presses or journals are those that don't make extra money, but rather take it. These are endowed awards given to the "best" poem published or the best book published in the journal or press that year. There is no entry fee, and therefore no money is generated. That's why these highly honorable contests are usually endowed. Our publishing world is in a real pickle.

Judith Kitchen On Contests

Since my press (State Street Press) publishes chapbooks and has a contest, I clearly think that contests allow editors to see more manuscripts than they might otherwise receive—and better ones. I believe that it *is* possible to be read, and published, by someone who does not know you and where there is no influence other than the quality of the poem.

David Citino on Contests

Whether Miss America or The Great Marion County Bake-Off, the Guggenheim Fellowship competition or the Thursday-Night Wet T-Shirt Contest or Hunk-of-the-Month Challenge, contests are odious, I sometimes feel; but it's also true that the spirit of competition can sometimes elicit from us—writers as well as anyone else—our best work. Entering a competition we must keep our wits about us at the same time we try to put our best feet forward. We need to believe that we can win, but at the same time we must bear in mind that we may lose for any number of reasons but probably not because we come up short and fail somehow as human beings. Every one of us knows a fellow writer or two who seems consumed by a competitive compulsiveness, an inability to take delight in the good fortune of another or to approach life in any other way than to see the success of a fellow writer as a diminishment of the self. This is unfortunate: a sure-fire guarantee that one's career will bring little joy, no matter what level of success is attained. As for the question of whether we should try our work (and our luck) in any given field of competition, I say "Why not?!" We can't truly excel if we don't extend ourselves. As the great competitor Wayne Gretsky is fond of saying, "100% of all the shots you don't take, don't go in."

Ruth Daigon On Contest Abuses

There are so many operators out there. Even if they're finally exposed, which sometimes happens, dozens more spring up like warriors from the dragon's teeth. Some of the abuses:

1. Most magazines have funding problems. One solution is to run a contest requiring a submission fee. Some charge $3 to $10 a poem and if by some stroke of luck you win, the prize is far too little compared with money taken in by the sponsor. It's a case of the promoters exploiting poets' hunger for recognition.

This kind of publication does not add to anyone's professional stature.

2. Watch out for the contest where everyone wins. It's a marketing device to sell books at inflated prices. They may have grandiose titles, something like *Literary Celebrations of Immortal Poetry*. When and if your free copy arrives you may find the table of contents missing, sloppy editing and a poorly constructed book. The publisher will certainly offer big bargains if you buy multiple copies, a sure sign that you've been had.

3. Sometimes sponsors have already made their decision long before the contest has even been announced and are merely raising funds to publish the poet of their choice. This may occur with perfectly respectable organizations.

4. You'll read ads urging you to submit poems for consideration. No reading fees. When you receive your acceptance letter, don't give way to unbounded joy. Virtually all entries are accepted hinging on your willingness to pay the sometimes exorbitant publication charges.

5. You should also know that the judges of these contests are often biased in their choices. Most of them teach at institutions, do workshops or have connections with other poets whose work they recognize. A significant number of judges' students find themselves on the winners list.

However, be assured, that despite widespread chicanery, there are legitimate outlets for working poems. They can be found in *Poets & Writers, The Poetry Society of America's Bulletin, Pen American Center's Grants And Awards, CLMP*'s reviews, *Poet's Market* and many other trustworthy sources. The prize may be important ($250.00 and up) but more important is the reputation of the contest's sponsors. If you want to be sure, *Poets & Writers* has an 800 number and you can certainly make inquiries about the ads they carry.

Recommended Assignments

All Levels

1. Research the contest market by following the ten tips provided at the end of this chapter. Then analyze your inventory of poems, find suitable ones to submit to the contests of your choice, and take your chances.

2. After results are announced in the contests you entered above, study winning entries or request copies of them. Compare your poems with the winning ones. Record your thoughts in your journal and ask yourself what you would change about your submissions if you had to do it over again. Would you send in a different poem? Pay more attention to the judge?

3. When the same contests are conducted again, re-read your journal entries and resubmit. Continue this process until you win, remembering that persistence is a key factor in any competition.

Chapter Four

Marketing Poems

Publishing poems is the purpose of writing poetry. Of course, we all know we write because we're compelled by other aspects of our lives that drive us mad from within, but once having served those clamoring voices, publishing the poem is a definite next. Without publication, there is no poem except for the poet and a few patient friends who might consent to listen or read. So it is important we get those words out onto a printed page. Otherwise, we are just talking to the wall.

—Laurel Speer

Three Phases of Marketing Poems

WHEN A POET commits words to a page, the act itself suggests a desire to share vision and verse with an audience. Composing a poem is half the battle. Publishing it completes the process, putting the muse in the public domain. Publication has three phases:

1. *Researching the markets.* [Purchasing basic directories, identifying publications, requesting sample copies, and reading magazines in the library.]

2. *Preparing a submission.* [Printing standard manuscripts, composing brief cover letters, using proper envelopes and postage, and maintaining files of poems and logs of mailing dates.]

3. *Dealing with editors.* [Querying magazines, filing and deciphering rejection slips, following etiquette, composing contributor's notes, and proofreading galleys.]

Many poets waste time making mistakes as they learn about the publishing process by trial and error. That often results in feelings of inadequacy as a poet. However, by following standard procedures, you can decrease the number of standard rejections. To do so, we'll tackle each element of the marketing process and then demystify it. Every poet has an obligation to publish verse. Other than doing readings, this is the only way for your work to reach an audience. Thus, if you have already joined a workshop, done a reading, or entered a contest, you should have plenty of poems by now to submit to magazines. Here's how.

Researching the Markets

Successful poets use one or more basic directories to become familiar with markets. Among the best are *Poet's Market* (Writer's Digest Books), with more than 1,700 listings; *International Directory of Little Magazines and Small Presses* (Dustbooks), with about 5,000 entries; and the handy *Directory of Literary Magazines* (Moyer Bell Limited), with about 500 magazines. Directories come and go, so be sure to check the reference sections of book stores and libraries to see what is available. Typically, each directory features data about specific publications with the bulk of listings devoted to small press and literary magazines, the biggest publishers of contemporary poetry. Simply read the listings and decide which magazines publish types of poetry similar to your own. You might want to identify possible publications by noting:

- The style that editors prefer (rhymed, metered, free verse, lyric, narrative, dramatic, etc.)
- The select topic (love, nature, political, war, environmental, etc.)
- The desired length (long, short, no length requirements)

Because most directories are annual, poets also should subscribe to or consult freelance periodicals like *Writer's Digest* to keep up with new markets or to record changes with old ones. Other than that, the directories are quite complete. You should use them to isolate about 20 magazines so that you can order sample copies or research them in the library.

Poets who send work without reading or researching magazines take a hit-and-miss approach to marketing, stalling their careers, wasting their supplies and postage, and trying their patience. Although directories often contain valuable editorial information, use them as leads to locate publications and later as references to locate addresses. If you don't, you are flirting with failure. A case in point:

A few years ago, typical listings for *The Hollins Critic* stated that editor John Rees Moore used short poems with interesting forms or content. *Strike One:* That's hardly enough information to go on when deciding whether to submit work. Moreover, all the directories described this 7-by-10 periodical as having 20 pages with a modest circulation ranging from 550 to 850. *Strike Two:* This in no way adequately described its handsome appearance and reputation for publishing powerful, lucid poems on expensive paper. *Strike Three:* If you failed to keep up with marketing data about *The Hollins Critic* in that year, by reading freelance writing magazines, you would not have known that the magazine was temporarily overstocked with poetry. Three strikes, and the poet's out. But the manuscript still isn't at a magazine whose editor will give your poems a close reading.

Preparing a Submission

After you have perused sample copies or studied publications in the library, you should have located at least a dozen magazines whose content and format are in keeping with your tastes. Now you should prepare a standard manuscript, usually three to five poems, typed or printed one poem to a page, single-spaced, (no dot-matrix or fancy fonts) on 20-pound 25% cotton white stock. Although you may use cheaper paper or photocopies, nothing compares to the crisp professional look of black ink on good bond. Moreover, single-spacing poems saves paper, eliminates irregular spacing between stanzas, and helps an editor visualize the shape of each poem on the printed page.

Before you begin typing or printing your poems, be sure to leave at least one-inch margins at the top and bottom and sides of the page. Your name and address should appear at the upper left- or right-hand corner. The title of your poem should appear in all caps or in initial caps about six lines underneath, flush left. (Flushing the name and address *right,* and the title and poem left, leaves an attractive white area on the page, enhancing the look.) Putting the title in all caps or initial caps distinguishes it from the first line of your poem, which should follow one line below the title. Also put a line of space between any stanzas. (See Illustration No. 1 at the end of this chapter.)

If your poem is longer than a page, you need to indicate that on each additional page of the poem. At the top left margin of each additional page, type your name (the address is optional) and underneath that, in parentheses, a key word from the title of the poem along with the page number and stanza information:

Michael Bugeja
(BLACKOUT, page 2, begin new stanza)

Or:

Michael Bugeja
(BLACKOUT, page 2, continue stanza)

You need to put your name, title of poem, and page number

on continuing pages in case they become separated during handling. (Stanza information also helps the editor visualize the shape of the poem as it continues from one page to the next.) After you have provided the above information, drop six lines and continue the poem.

Putting a copyright notice alongside your poem is optional. Stanley Lindberg, editor of *The Georgia Review* and co-author of the book *The Nature of Copyright,* says, "You can put the copyright symbol on your poem, but you don't need to. You own the copyright at the moment of creation, and as an editor, I know that. If a poet feels better adding the notice, okay: use the notice. It usually won't influence an editor one way or the other."

I don't recommend using the symbol. Instead I advise poets to stop worrying about their poems being stolen and to invest that energy in putting together a professional-looking manuscript. When you prepare a manuscript, it goes without saying that no word should be misspelled and that each line should be grammatically correct, poetic license notwithstanding. Further, in the computer age with its word processing and spell checking, editors are used to clean copy, so do not pencil in any corrections on the page. Keep in mind that while a clean manuscript never guarantees an acceptance, it *does* indicate that the poet has respect for the submitted work. Most editors will honor that with a close reading, increasing your chances.

After you have typed or printed three to five poems, arrange them in a tantalizing order. Some poets like to put their best poem first, to make an impression, while others build slowly to their last, most impressive work. Some poets like to put poems about serious subjects first and then end with a light, short lyric. Others include poems related to one theme while some opt to send a sample of different styles of verse. In the end, the choice is yours. While there is no "correct" order of poems to serve all editors, evidence of any continuity helps editors get more involved with a submission, again assuring a closer reading and increasing your chances.

Finally, after you have established the order of poems, fold them into thirds as you would a letter to fit into a Size 9 envelope, or the one you will use as your SASE. Never staple a manuscript. Some editorial assistants prefer that you use a paper clip before folding the manuscript, but clips leave marks when poems are returned, giving a submission a soiled look. (Buying boxes of clips also is a waste of money.) Ideally, you should get to use a clean manuscript on sturdy bond paper two or three times before having to type or print a new batch. If poems are returned with stains or creases in the paper, you may want to retype or print again. In any case, use good judgment. Don't make new copies of poems if the paper is still crisp or only slightly soiled. Paper costs money, too, and wasting paper in today's world is environmentally unsound. So recycle soiled poems or give them to friends.

For that reason, I don't like wasting paper for cover letters stating the obvious: "Please consider the enclosed manuscript." When I include them, I like to introduce myself as a contributing editor of *Writer's Digest* or mention some other aspect of my life and work. Moreover, if I have spent time researching a particular market or know the editor or publication, I might note a poem or two that I liked in a back issue of the magazine or add something personal and appropriate.

As a rule, check directories like *Poet's Market* to see if a specific editor requests or discourages cover letters. If you decide to write one, use blank paper without the tacky personalized letterhead indicating that your title is "poet," a dead giveaway that you are an amateur probably submitting a substandard manuscript. Simply address the poetry editor at the magazine and use his or her full name after the saluation; do not guess at courtesy titles—"Mr.," "Miss," "Mrs.," or "Ms."—or appear informal by using first names: "Dear John" or "Dear Jane." The cover letter should be no longer than 100 words, stating the nature of the submission and listing any publication credits, with a quick, appreciative exit. (See Illustration No. 2 at the end of this chapter.)

If you have any doubt about writing a cover letter, resist the urge. The absence of a cover letter may actually benefit you, especially if you have no prior credits. The submission of a professional-looking manuscript will make it appear as if you have published poems before. But if you write a cover letter, fold it in thirds and place it atop your folded manuscript, putting both and the stamped Size 9 self-addressed envelope in a properly addressed Size 10 envelope with adequate postage. You don't want to guess at postage, but a rule of thumb is one first class stamp on a Size 10 envelope will pay for three pages of poetry, a cover letter, and an SASE. You usually can mail four pages of poetry without a cover letter but occasionally editors will stuff bulky subscription cards with rejected manuscripts, fouling your best postal intentions. Postal scales available at most office supply shops are inexpensive, accurate, and a good investment.

Finally, do not enclose anything else with a poetry submission. As a former poetry editor, I have received manuscripts with personal photographs, illustrations, frames, and other unmentionables. Such items tell an editor more about the poet than the poet's work, again making you appear amateurish.

Professionals stick to the basics, and the basics include bookkeeping. Once your manuscript is in the mail, you need to log information about where and when you sent individual poems. So always make copies of your poems and keep them in a file folder with a "log" or ledger for quick access. This is simply a piece of paper or file on computer disk reminding you where and when you sent submissions. The log should list the name of each poem in your inventory, the intended market, the date sent, and response. (See Illustration No. 3 at the end of this chapter.) Once your manuscript is mailed and logged, concentrate on composing more poems until you have to deal again with editors.

Some magazines are notoriously slow in making responses, taking as long as a year to reject or accept a poem. That's why many poets simultaneously submit their work to several magazines, a practice I discourage, because it complicates bookkeeping and sometimes necessitates awkward correspondences. Editors assume that all submitted work is original and not previously published elsewhere. Many also assume that your poems are not being considered at other magazines. So if you are planning to make simultaneous submissions, consult directories like *Poet's Market* to ascertain editorial policies. For instance, some editors have no qualms about considering poems that also are being considered by other editors. Others consider this an insult. Increasingly, however, many poets are sending manuscripts to more than one editor at a time. They believe, rightly so, that editors in general are too slow to respond and that the market for poems is limited at best. Authors feel that a manuscript of 3-5 poems sent to two or more editors stands a better chance of acceptance.

But there are drawbacks as well. First, making simultaneous submissions costs money, time, and supplies. Moreover, when an editor accepts a poem that is out at two or more places, the poet has to telephone or write the other editors immediately, withdrawing his or her work. If this happens to you, don't tell the editors that one particular poem has been accepted and others rejected at a rival magazine, so they should consider the remaining "rejected" ones. Withdraw all poems at once. If asked to explain, tell the truth and suffer the consequences.

Finally, here are a few personal reasons why you may not want to engage in simultaneous submissions. If you are not publishing regularly, you probably will collect rejections quicker while still perfecting your craft. That can be discouraging. If you already are publishing regularly, you stand a greater chance of having poems accepted at several places at once. Why taint your good name? All poets share one virtue: patience.

If you are unsure, but leaning toward simultaneous submissions, pick a prestigious magazine where your chances, at best, will be slim, and another more realistic small-press or literary magazine. The high prestige magazine usually receives thousands upon thousands of poems each year and takes only a few. So you will probably be rejected anyway, eliminating the worry about being *accepted* simultaneously. (On the rare chance that you are, write a letter of apology to the lesser magazine and, if the editor is upset by this, cross the magazine off your list of intended markets.)

Submitting simultaneously to magazines is only one way to deal with editors who are slow responding to your work. You can also write them a letter and ask about the status of your manuscript. (For the format, see Illustration No. 4 at the end of this chapter.) Response times differ at each magazine, so check listings for such information in standard directories. Generally, you probably should contact a tardy editor after 20 weeks or so. (Don't telephone.)

To query an editor, simply check your log and inform him or her when you sent your poems, listing individual titles. Ask the editor when he or she anticipates making a decision. Remember, editors often keep a manuscript in-house longer when it is under serious consideration, so don't press the staff to make a quick decision. As always, include a return postcard or Size 9 stamped envelope for the reply.

After you mail your query, jot down the date in your personal log for the poems in question. If the editor fails to respond to your query or to return your poems after four to six more weeks, send the magazine a postcard informing the staff when you sent your manuscript, when you sent your query with no reply, and that you are withdrawing the manuscript. Do not include a return postcard or SASE.

While it is true that poets often send second query letters hoping that editors will respond, especially after six months, there is no need to tie up your poems longer. The magazine is probably understaffed, swamped with submissions, or temporarily not reading manuscripts (especially during the summer). Write off the submission as a "business loss" and try another market. Never respond personally to an editor with an angry letter complaining about the delay. Again, you'll be branded as a beginner. Some editors even keep a file of "problem poets," alerting editorial assistants who open the mail.

Most editors will reply promptly to queries and submissions, returning your work with a rejection slip. While I publish almost every poem I compose, my logs indicate that sometimes the process can take 10 years. For instance, one poem written in 1982 was sent to 42 magazines, was accepted in 1990, and published in 1992. Prepare to be rejected. I receive six rejections for every acceptance and keep a bulky file of slips for marketing purposes. Some rejections explain the best time to submit work. Some report new addresses, editorial changes, or upcoming thematic issues.

When an editor sends me an unsigned rejection, I decipher the message to see if the magazine is interested in my verse. Typically, magazines have two kinds of unsigned rejections: standard and encouraging. The standard reads something like this—"Thank you for sending your work, but we regret that we are unable to use it"—and the encouraging one like this: "Although we have decided against using this manuscript, we were interested in it and would be glad to see more of your work."

Don't read too much into the standard type of rejection. Some magazines only stock one style, or perhaps the editorial assistant has run out of encouraging rejection slips. But if you receive a personal note or response, take it seriously. A personal rejection includes anything scribbled on the unsigned slip, even the words "Sorry" or "Thank you." Some editors know that such phrases encourage writers to send more work while others are just being courteous. I like working with encouraging *or* courteous editors, so I'll usually submit another manuscript to the publication in a month or two. (Generally, unless asked to do so, don't send more than two or three submissions to the same magazine in the course of a year.) Here are some other quick items that concern poet-editor etiquette:

1. *Lost Manuscripts.* One or two manuscripts out of thousands in the typical reading cycle of a top journal ever get lost, according to David Baker, a poet and magazine editor. "You're going so fast through piles of poems it's bound to happen," he observes, "but again, rarely."

It can happen, however. If you have queried an editor and he or she has no record of your submission—or doesn't respond at all to your query (with SASE)—consider the manuscript lost and submit elsewhere.

2. *No Rejection Slip.* Occasionally manuscripts are returned without a rejection slip, as if editors didn't want to waste one on a poet of your caliber. What message is the magazine trying to send? Answer: none. Editorial offices get busy with phones ringing and people interrupting and staffers losing track of the routine: slip in a rejection, lick or sponge the SASE, toss it in the mail bin. Sometimes the slip just doesn't make it in the envelope. Ignore it.

3. *Missing Poems.* Occasionally a poem or two is missing when a manuscript is returned with or without a rejection slip. Again, it's probably an oversight but this one needs to be addressed. The first time this happened to me I thought, simply, that the editorial assistant neglected to stuff the poem with others. I sent the poem out again and it was accepted by another magazine. Imagine my surprise, and the second editor's, when the poem eventually appeared simultaneously in two journals.

If your log indicates that a poem sent to a magazine hasn't been returned with others in a manuscript, write the editor a brief business letter informing him or her about the matter. Tell the editor that you presume the poem has been rejected. There's no need to enclose an SASE for a response, but do copy your letter for your files in case the poem, like mine, appears later in two magazines. The copy of your letter is evidence that you followed standard procedure and an editor didn't.

4. *Mishandled Manuscripts.* It's rare, but sometimes you'll receive somebody else's rejected poems in your envelope or somebody else's *acceptance* (as happened once to me). In such case, send the editor a postcard noting what happened and request further instructions (along with their SASE if they want you to return the mishandled items).

5. *Nasty Rejections.* Sometimes editors will sting you with a word or two about a submission. One poet I know sent this note with his manuscript: "This is my best shot." He received a rejection that read: "Fire when your gun is loaded." Another poet got back her manuscript balled-up as if editors hated the contents so much that, poor souls, they couldn't help themselves.

When this happens, do not fire back a nastier letter to the editor (or ball up your sample copy of the magazine) but do share the rejection or incident with other poets so that they won't send there. If the offending editor works for a magazine listed in a standard directory, photocopy the rejection or briefly describe the offense in a quick letter and send either to the editor of that directory. (Don't libel the editor or protest emotionally.) Simply state—"For your information"—and let the directory worry about the matter. When I edited *Poet's Market,* we would keep such letters in a file and consider removing magazines from our lists upon receiving several complaints.

So much for bad news. Sooner or later you are going to hit your target market. When you do, the editor will send you an informal or formal contract for your poems. (See Illustrations Nos. 5 and 6 at the end of this chapter.) An informal contract is a letter or note accepting your verse. The editor is assuming that it is original and unpublished and is contracting for the right to publish your poem before anyone else in a U.S. or Canadian periodical. Typically, the copyright reverts to you upon publication or is held by the magazine and reverts upon request. A formal contract spells out in legal language what rights are being bought and what is expected of you as author. Most formal contracts purchase the right to print your poem first, with the copyright reverting to you after publication or again, upon request.

Many formal contracts reserve the right to reprint your work in anthologies or special editions. Some contracts require you to ask permission before reprinting your poem in any future collection. Terms are clearly spelled out. In more than 15 years of publishing poems, I have not encountered a contract that I did not sign.

In an acceptance letter, many editors will ask that you send back a contributor's note with the contract. If this represents your first publication, say so in the note and add a sentence or two about what you do for a living or some other interesting tidbit (preferably related to writing). Make the note brief and informative, never coy or cute. Before composing one, check sample copies of the magazine to get a sense of the style. Here is the contributor's note for my first publication in the Spring 1981 issue of *Texas Review*:

> Michael J. Bugeja, an assistant professor of journalism at Oklahoma State University, recently received honorable mention in the *Writer's Digest* poetry contest.

After you mail your contract and contributor's note, you'll either receive a copy of the magazine with your poem or galleys for you to proofread and return. If you get a contributor's copy first, proofreading was done at the magazine. If you get the galleys, don't attempt to revise your poem—some editors will charge typesetting fees if you do—but correct any typos or printing mistakes. (Consult a standard dictionary or editing text if you do not know proofreading symbols.) Proofing errors often overlooked concern the spelling of the author's name, a word in the title, capitalization, punctuation (especially missing or reversed quotation marks), missing lines, lines broken in the wrong place, and misspellings. (See Illustration No. 7 at the end of this chapter.) When you proofread the galleys, consult error-free copies of your poems and triple-check each word and mark on the page. Then have someone else you know, preferably another writer, read the galleys and originals. Finally, read both again before returning the proofs within 48 hours of receipt.

There is no need to send editors a letter when you return the galleys, but many appreciate a note of thanks after your poem appears in a magazine. Again, be patient. It is not uncommon for the publishing process to take several years from the time you first researched a market. But if you have seen the process through the three phases of publication explained in this chapter, you can ease back with your contributor's copy, knowing your verse is being shared with readers and is setting standards for other writers.

Illustrations

1. Typed Poem in Standard Format

2. Mailing Log for Individual Poems

3. Brief Cover Letter

4. Sample Query Letter

5. Informal Contract

6. Formal Contract

7. Proofed Galley

ILLUSTRATION #1: Typed Poem in Standard Format

[1-inch margins top, bottom of page & left, right of page]

Michael J. Bugeja
E.W. Scripps Hall   [Name and address flush left or right]
Ohio University
Athens, Ohio 45701

[6 lines of white space between name/address & title of poem]

THE CARPE DIEM BLUES

The lover's complaint yodel-lady-hoos
In the Alps. He would like to clear the air
But has a case of the carpè diem blues.

He envisions his Lorelie in *lederhose,*
Oblivious of clothes that sirens wear.
The lover's complaint yodel-lady-hoos

Amid vast mountaintops of spruce and snow,
Hardly an oracle to lament an affair:
He has a case of the carpè diem blues.

This alarms him like a roost of cuckoos
In the shops and chalets tolling the hour.
The lover's complaint yodel-lady-hoos

And cracks the ice the way Valkyries do
In Valhalla, warbling arias there.
He has a case of the carpè diem blues.

Voices come back to him, haunting the hollows
Of his hickory-dickory heart, beyond repair.
The lover's complaint yodel-lady-hoos.
He has a case of the carpè diem blues.

ILLUSTRATION #2: Brief Cover Letter

E.W. Scripps Hall
Ohio University
Athens, Ohio 45701

[5 lines of white space between address & date]

January 5, 1993
[2 lines of white space between address & salutation]

Hilda Raz, Editor-in-Chief
Prairie Schooner
201 Andrews Hall
University of Nebraska
Lincoln, Nebraska 68588-0334
[1 line of white space between address & salutation]
Dear Hilda Raz:
[1 line of white space between salutation & first paragraph]
I read the Fall 1993 special poetry issue of *Prairie Schooner* and particularly enjoyed the poems of Ted Kooser, Marnie Bullock, and Rafael Campo. I thought I would send you a submission of five poems from a book-length manuscript in progress titled *Talk*.
[1 line of white space between paragraphs]
My work has previously appeared in *The Kenyon Review, Poetry, TriQuarterly*, and *The Georgia Review*, among others. I teach writing and ethics at Ohio University and once worked in Lincoln as a reporter for United Press International. So I know your city well.

Thank you for your time and consideration.
[1 line of white space last paragraph & closing]
Sincerely,

[4 lines of white space between closing & name]

Michael J. Bugeja
(614) 555-3737

[Titles of poems with place sent, date of mailing, date of response]

STORMY: Paris Review 1-89-92, rejected 3-29-92; Texas Review 4-5-92, rejected 6-16-92; Crazyhorse 7-10-92, no response as of 12-8-92, query sent, rejected 2-10-93; Amelia 2-14-93, rejected 5-23-93; Laurel Review 5-28-93, rejected 9-20-93; Chariton Review 10-2-93, rejected 12-3-93; Ascent 1-6-94

THE TALK: Southern Review 3-3-94, rejected 5-6-94; TriQuarterly 6-1-94, rejected—not reading until fall—6-30-94; Missouri Review, 7-5-94

THAW: Indiana Review 2-14-89, rejected 5-2-89; New England Review 5-4-89, rejected 1-15-90; Hawai'i Review 2-20-90, no response as of 6-1-90, query sent 6-24-90, manuscript passed to incoming staff according to editor, accepted 10-1-90.

CARPE DIEM BLUES: Georgia Review 10-3-89, rejected 2-8-90; Paris Review, 2-19-90, rejected 5-23-90; Hudson Review 5-24-90, rejected 7-14-90; Raritan Review, 7-20-90, rejected 9-2-90; Gettysburg Review 9-4-90, rejected 1-12-91; Missouri Review, 1-20-91, rejected 3-15-91; Poetry 3-16-91, rejected 6-14-91; Southwest Review 6-15-91, rejected 8-12-91; PN Review 8-15-91, rejected 11-28-91; Hellas 12-3-91, rejected 3-23-92; The Formalist, 4-1-92, rejected 6-6-92; American Poetry Review 6-8-92, rejected 10-3-92; South Coast Poetry Journal 10-5-92, rejected 12-18-92, The Lyric 12-19-92, rejected 2-3-93; Blue Unicorn 2-8-93, accepted 4-23-93

E.W. Scripps Hall
Ohio University
Athens, Ohio 45701

June 24, 1990

John Gesang, Poetry Editor
Hawaii Review
University of Hawaii at Manoa
1733 Donaghho Road
Honolulu, Hawaii 96822

Dear John Gesang:

On February 20, 1990, I sent you these poems: "Thaw," "Love, Hate: The Life We Learn," and "When I Feel Your Soul, I Reach For You With These Arms."

Can you please let me know whether you have received my manuscript and, if so, when you anticipate making a decision?

Feel free to keep the poems longer if they are still under active consideration.

Sincerely,

Michael J. Bugeja
(614) 555-3737

DEPAUL UNIVERSITY

Poetry East
802 West Belden Avenue
Chicago, Illinois 60614-3214
312/362-5114

June 16, 1991

Dear Michael Bugeja

I've read your poems with pleasure and would like to accept the following for publication in POETRY EAST:

ENERGY

Your poems will appear in a future issue of POETRY EAST. You will receive galley proofs shortly before publication.

POETRY EAST is copyrighted in its own name, but rights (except for non-exclusive rights to reprint in future POETRY EAST publications) revert to author on publication. Copyright is retained by author, but we ask that POETRY EAST be acknowledged in any future publication.

At your earliest convenience, please send us a brief biographical note for our Contributors file. Please include your complete address, home and work phone numbers, and your social security number.

We appreciate your offering us the opportunity to present your work in POETRY EAST.

Sincerely,

Richard Jones

Michael--Hoped you liked the suggestions--I think "Energy" is a great poem. Glad to have you in our pages again! All best,

Auburn University
Auburn, Alabama 36849-5202

CONSENT TO PUBLISH

Auburn University (the Publisher) is pleased to have the privilege of publishing your contribution to the *Southern Humanities Review* (the SHR), entitled ___"Prognosis of the Pupa"___ (poem) _____

_____(the Contribution).

You, as Author, and the Publisher hereby agree as follows:

1. Whereas the Publisher is undertaking to publish the Contribution in the SHR, you hereby grant and assign exclusively to the Publisher the entire literary property and all rights of whatever kind in the Contribution, and every part thereof, during the full term of copyright in the United States of America and elsewhere.

2. Upon publication of the Contribution, the Publisher grants you, without charge, the right to republish the Contribution in revised or unrevised form, in any language, in any volume consisting wholly of your own work, provided that each such use shall carry the proper copyright notice of the original publication of the Contribution by the Publisher in the SHR.

3. You represent and warrant to the Publisher that the Contribution is original and that you are the sole author of it and have full power to make this agreement; that the Contribution has not been previously published, in whole or in part, except as you have advised the Publisher in writing; and that you shall indemnify the Publisher and the SHR against any losses and other expenses by reason of any claim brought in violation of this warranty.

4. The Publisher will protect copyright in the Contribution by registering copyright to the SHR issue in which it appears.

5. You understand and agree that all details of publishing, selling, and licensing the Contribution shall be under the control of the SHR as directed by the Publisher.

6. Should any fee be collected by the Publisher or the SHR from a license to reprint or translate all or any portion of the Contribution in a reader, anthology, or any other forms of publication; and should such fee amount to twenty-five dollars ($25.00) or more, the Publisher and the SHR will make a reasonable attempt to locate you and to pay you fifty percent (50%) of the fee money collected, such payment to be made within six (6) months of receipt of the fee by the Publisher or the SHR; and the balance of any such fee shall be paid to the SHR. If any fee is collected by the Publisher or the SHR in an amount less than twenty-five ($25.00), no portion shall be paid to you, but the entire amount shall be paid to the SHR to help defray publication, administrative, and editorial costs.

7. You will be given an opportunity to read and correct proofs of the Contribution, but if proofs are not returned on schedule, production and publication may proceed without your approval of proof. The Publisher will charge you the cost of any changes, excluding typographical errors, made by you in proof.

If the terms of this agreement are satisfactory to you, please sign and date this agreement and return the original copy to the Publisher at the address specified below. Please be sure to fill in the title of your Contribution in the space above. *We are unable to publish your Contribution without a signed copy of this form.*

___Michael Bugeja___
Author's signature   Michael J. Bugeja

___Dec. 3, 1990___   ___(000)000-0000___
Date   Phone

___000-00-0000___
Social Security Number

___000 Rolling Hills Dr.___
Current Address

___Athens, OH 45701___

Return form to:

The Editors
  Southern Humanities Review
9088 Haley Center
Auburn University, Alabama 36849-5202

(add accent)

The Carpè Diem Blues

(t/)
The lover's complain/yodel-lady-hoos
In the Alps. He would like to clear the air
But has a case of the carpè diem blues.

He envisions his Lorelie in <u>lederhose,</u> *(italics)*
Oblivious of clothes that sirens wear.
The lover's complaint yodel-lady-hoos

Amid vast mountaintops of spruce and snow,
Hardly an oracle to lament an affair:
He has a case of the carpè diem blues.

This alarms him like a roost of cuckoos
In the shops and chalets tolling the hour.
The lover's complaint yodel-lady-hoos

And cracks the ice the way Valkyries do
In Valhalla, warbling arias there.
He has a case of the carpè diem blues.

Voices come back to him, haunting the hollows
Of his hickory-dickory heart, beyond repair.
The lover's complaint yodel-lady-hoos.
He has a case of the carpè diem blus.   *(X)*

Guidebook

Susan Ludvigson's "Dream" Publication

I rely heavily on dreams for inspiration as well as for imagery. But never until this week did dreams figure into my ideas about publication. But I dreamed a couple of nights ago that a young man came into my father's old cafe (defunct since the late 1940s) to talk to my father (also defunct) and my mother and me. After chatting with my parents, he offered me a credit card issued by a prominent literary magazine—one I hadn't thought of sending poems to for years. In the dream it seemed a marvelous idea—a brilliant new source of revenue for small magazines. Upon waking, that didn't seem like such a hot idea but I thought I would send that magazine some poems. And I will. I wish there were time to report whether dreams are reliable sources for knowing where to send poems, but I suspect that was the message of the dream. We'll see.

Jonathan Holden On The Future Of Poems

Poetry is going to be, increasingly, about media and the mediated nature of human experience—more of Wallace Stevens's project, but less implicit than it is in Stevens. I just finished reading, in *The New Yorker,* a fascinating essay on Katherine Ann Power, the radical who was accessory to the death of a Boston police officer in 1970, fled, lived under an assumed name, established a successful life in Covallis, Oregon, and recently, out of nagging guilt, turned herself in. It was more interesting than any poem I've read in recent memory, and it confirmed my realization that, in writing, journalism is where the real action is.

The real life story of O.J. Simpson is great art, almost ready-made. Poetry is going to have to be about T.V. news, about the movies. It's going to have to find a way to access their subject matter and then handle it in a way these media can't, probably by accessing the inner lives of the characters involved. But this is what novels do, right? Why try to do it in verse? Or are poets going to be left doing, as the late William Stafford said, "piddling little tasks . . . crochet work?"

I don't know the answers. . . . I think also that the dramatic monologue is going to stage—is staging—a major return as a viable form. This, I think, is inevitable in the ecology of media and genre, wherein each medium or genre seeks its maximum potentiality with respect to the others.

Recommended Assignments

Beginning Level

Research your publications and prepare your submissions according to steps outlined in this chapter. Record your submissions in your personal business log and keep track of them. Deal with editors in a cordial and professional manner and be patient through every phase of the marketing process.

Intermediate and Advanced Levels

1. By this time you should have many poems making the rounds, perhaps with a few acceptances. You also should have new poems ready for submission. Perhaps an editor has expressed interest in seeing more of your work. If so, send another manuscript. Keep rotating your manuscripts from one select editor to another so that each publication becomes familiar with the range of your work.

2. You should continue to expand the market for your verse by researching new publications. As your inventory grows, you want to become familiar with more and more outlets. Here's a rule of thumb: For every manuscript of 3-5 poems, you should have at least four possible magazines in mind. So if you have 30 poems in your inventory, or six to ten manuscripts, you should be familiar with 24 to 40 potential publications. Using that formula, figure out your ratio of poems to potential markets. Research new publications as needed.

Chapter Five

Revising for Publication

Years ago I used to fear that an editor's input somehow compromised my ownership of the poem, but now I understand that, if my signature is burned deeply into the shaping process, it will govern any influence.

—R.T. Smith

The Final Edit

So FAR YOU have learned the basics of marketing and have been submitting your work regularly to contests and magazines. Perhaps you have also joined a poetry workshop and now receive critiques on a regular basis. Chances are, you have been listening to suggestions about improving your poems, but also have been calling the shots, experiencing no real pressure to revise your verse. The critique that matters most has yet to come.

When a poet sends manuscripts to magazines, sooner or later he or she will receive a letter (instead of a rejection slip) asking for a final edit. Sometimes the edit is minor—a few word-changes here or there in a poem, or maybe a new title—and sometimes the edit is more substantial: the elimination of a stanza, the revision of a theme, or the rejiggering of rhyme (or even form) in a more traditional work. Frequently the edit is optional, and the editor will take the poem with or without suggested changes. Other times acceptance of a poem depends on the revision in question. Occasionally the editor knows exactly what he or she wants, proposes mandatory changes, and asks the poet to approve them . . . or send the work elsewhere.

In sum, editors know their audiences (or their own tastes). Poets who know how to revise for publication usually end up with better poems and more acceptance letters. On the other hand, suggested revisions are just that—*suggested*—and poets may refuse to do or to approve them.

No one can tell you what you should do, if an editor asks you for a final edit. Each case depends on three factors: the poem, the poet, and the editor. In this chapter, however, I have taken examples of rewrite requests from my files when I was an editor of a literary magazine and from my correspondence now as a poet, illustrating the various types of changes that editors suggest and poets consider. Then I will suggest some criteria to help you decide how (and if) you should proceed to execute a final edit.

Such a request may come to you at any time. When it does, all manner of questions will swim through your head. To wit:

- Do you change a work that appeals to you?
- If you disagree with the editor's comments, do you still do the edit and go for the acceptance?
- Are the editor's instructions clear enough for you even to attempt the edit?
- Do you have the skill to accomplish it?
- Should you approve changes by an editor that interject his or her words into your poem?
- Whose poem is it anyway?

The best way to answer these questions is to analyze case studies so that you can see how other poets dealt with similar requests and to study poems that entail minor, significant, and major alterations. If you understand the process, you can make the important decisions independently.

Two Case Studies

In the 1980s, I was poetry editor for a national literary magazine at Oklahoma State University. Readers of *Cimarron Review* mostly were fiction and essay-lovers who did not appreciate too much obscurity in a poem. My assistant poetry editor and I shared the tastes of the audience; we didn't like obscurity, either. So when we found a poem that we thought our readers would enjoy, we asked ourselves basic questions:

1. Does the poem take a risk?
2. Would our readers enjoy or appreciate the topic and theme?
3. Can the poem be improved?

If the poet got by Questions 1 and 2, but not 3, he or she received a rewrite request.

Such was the case with Joan Halperin, a New York poet who sent us a work titled "Echoes." We found the piece exciting and thought our readers would be moved by its topic and theme, but we knew that her verse could be improved. Specifically, we believed it needed a descriptive title, better line breaks, and well-crafted stanzas, along with a bit of tightening here and there. We told Halperin that if she would do what amounted to a significant revision, we would be glad to reconsider her work.

Here is the rewrite that she sent us:

Traces

My father bends to me, his face
silvery onion skin.
In darkness, his whiskied breath
folds down on me
heavy as old comforters.

Nights, he allows himself to touch
my hair, my rounded shoulders
waiting for him to lift
my body to his chest.

Father whispers "darling, sweetheart mine."
I am a favored child, a glittering
girl. But tomorrow
in that grey coat that buttons
past his lips, he'll walk me
up to school

and disappear.
Buckles of his black galoshes
flapping castinets along the road
to the redbrick factory.

Traces of my nights
spread into days.
His face in ceiling cracks,
his contour etched in flaking
plaster in the gym.

I do not even hear the teacher
when she calls my name.
She orders me to find Australia
where borders have a meaning
and roads and rivers follow
separate paths.

My assistant and I still thought the title was weak and the
poem could be improved. Most editors reject at this juncture,
but we were attracted so much by Halperin's haunting voice
that we made the revisions ourselves and asked the poet to
approve them. Some editors only accept poems or suggest revi-
sions. Others take a more active role in the process, as we did at
Cimarron, especially when we wanted a submission for a certain
issue of the magazine and lacked the time to work with a poet.
We knew, of course, that such requests could turn off authors

who did not want an editor's words interjected into their verse. We also knew that other poets would be thankful that an editor took the time to analyze and make specific changes. (These were poets with whom we wanted to work anyway, so the process also helped us identify amiable writers.)

Here is the rewrite and letter of explanation that we sent Joan Halperin:

Fatherly Love: The Obsession

My father bends to me, his face
an onion skin: silvery. In darkness,
his whiskied breath folds down on me
heavy as old comforters. Nights,

he allows himself to touch me,
my hair, my rounded shoulders,
waiting for him to lift my body
to his chest. He whispers, "Darling,

sweetheart mine." I am the favored
child, glittering girl. But tomorrow
in that grey coat that buttons
past his lips, he'll walk me to school

and disappear, buckles of his black
galoshes flapping castinets
by the road to the redbrick factory.
Traces of nights smear into days:

his face in ceiling cracks, his figure
etched in the gym's flaked plaster.
I do not even hear the teacher
when she calls my name.

She orders me to find Australia
where borders have a meaning
and roads and rivers follow
separate paths.

~

Dear Joan:

Your revised poem has merit but still falls short of what I am looking for. However, I find it so moving, so well-thought-out, that I revised it for you in the form that we would accept for our journal.

Let me explain the revisions. The title of this poem is highly important. Your stanzas are more evocative than explicit and the title needs to add direction to how we read the poem. "Traces" is very weak, not only because you are withholding information from the reader but because it falls in that pattern of cliche titles: "Reflections," "Feelings," "Echoes," "Traces." Your line breaks need to augment meaning, again because your stanzas *suggest* rather than tell.

I've tried to do that wherever possible. I've used the colon as a device to push the poem out of the speaker. I've enjambed lines and stanzas (except the last one) because stanzas should have no boundaries either, in keeping with the poem's theme. The last stanza has the effect now of being broken off from the body of the poem, because the speaker suddenly is called to reality.

Whether or not you agree to these changes, I want to tell you I admire the content and risk you take in your work. You remind me a little bit of Sharon Olds, whom you may know from her books *Satan Says* and *The Dead and the Living*.

Sincerely,
Michael

Here is Halperin's reply:

Dear Michael,

I received your letter and revision of my poem. First let me thank you for your interest and time you took to help me. This poem has tremendous meaning for me and though I revised and tinkered with it, until now, I felt it lacked a certain kind of substance and power I was looking to achieve. I accept and appreciate your revisions. I feel extremely satisfied.

I also want to thank you for your comment on my work. I thought you would be pleased at your own perception if I told you I wrote this poem as an "entry" poem to enter one of Sharon Olds' workshops at the "Y." I studied with her for about three months.

Sincerely,
Joan

Soon after we took Halperin's poem, we received a manuscript from Eve Shelnutt, an accomplished and esteemed poet. Again, we thought that the following lyric took risks, would please our readers, but could still be improved:

There Is A Streak Of Quiet Melancholy

There is a streak of quiet melancholy
in my sisters' spirits. The slightest
allusion to music brings tears to their
eyes though their intelligent faces
never change. Sometimes they agree
by signal when to cry, and instruments
take up their places at music stands.
Gondolas floated in the moonlit harbour
when our parents met; a slow recovery
was taking place. "Why do you stare so?"
our mother asked, and Father, with a
thousand caresses, rowed to shore.
We must realize that not a soul knows
who he really is. Calmly we must sit
at the organ bench when a storm breaks
and play the work we see open there.
Let us put down our napkins and stare
across the room. Who is rowing?
Yet when the music begins, slowly
they put their hands over their bowed heads.

We sent Shelnutt this letter:

Dear Eve,

We enjoyed your poems. We particularly liked "There is a Streak of Quiet Melancholy." In fact, if you are willing to revise it, we would like to see it again with more of your work.

Some guidelines:

1. Use the title to help tie the three aspects of your poem together. At best, you have a working title now that simply repeats the first line.

2. The first seven lines are good. I could quibble with line breaks but will hold off on that for now.

3. The next five lines don't work well for us. The imagery is fine, but the diction bogs down. Try to link the gondola section more with the first part. Metaphor, elaboration, and stanza break should help.

4. The next and final section of your poem returns us to the voice of the first part. The sentence "We must realize . . . / who he really is" is awkward. The next sentence comprising 2½ lines is good and of the caliber we want for the poem.

5. The final four lines should be revised to make the wonderful idea click in entirety.

I hope you will try a rewrite, but if not, please accept these comments only as an indicator of what we want for *Cimarron*. Certainly, your work here is publishable elsewhere.

Best,
Michael

We never heard back from her. A year later I left my post as poetry editor and took a job in the Journalism department at Ohio University. By coincidence, Eve Shelnutt had moved as well to the English department at the same university, and we became colleagues and later friends. So I asked her why she didn't send us a rewrite.

This is what she said:

"I didn't revise 'There is a Streak of Quiet Melancholy' as suggested because then, and since, I have been interested in sudden juxtapositions in my poems, as occurs with the line beginning 'Gondolas floated. . . .' I also didn't change 'We must realize that not a soul knows/ who he really is' because I was imagining the narrator talking plainly and deliberately to her sisters. Too, I wanted to suggest that the 'he' refers both to the father and to humankind. As for the title as the first line: Sometimes I like that repetition; not often, and when I use the repetition, I'm never sure why this time and not another. Always I quibble with myself when revising; generally, I leave what seems right intuitively; often, I will choose the more "raw" version. . . . I like for my poems to mirror the restlessness of my mind, its inconclusiveness."

In the case of Eve Shelnutt, her work did not suit our needs at *Cimarron* at the time. (It did suit the needs of other editors at dozens of magazines across the country.) We understood this, and so did the poet. And when we saw her work in print elsewhere, we were happy for Shelnutt because she had come so close with us. Editors usually are grateful when they reject good poems and then discover that they eventually found homes anyway.

Moreover, the case studies of Joan Halperin and Eve Shelnutt illustrate two important concepts on opposite ends of the spectrum. Halperin accepted our rewrite of her poem, and Shelnutt accepted the fact that *Cimarron Review* probably was not the best market for her alluring and elusive verse. Thus, rewrite requests not only help editors know poets with whom they would like to work, but vice versa: poets also infer information about editorial tastes. In a worst case scenario, Joan Halperin and Eve Shelnutt could have written us angry letters, the former damning our edits and the latter our suggested ones. Instead, Halperin ended up with an acceptance and Shelnutt, valuable marketing data about *Cimarron*. Both poets saved us, and themselves, energy and time.

Now let's look at case studies from my files as poet.

Optional and/or Mandatory Edits

In going through a decade's worth of correspondence, I found more than two dozen rewrite requests from editors. Some were optional; in other words, the poem was accepted as is, although editors asked me to change a word or phrase or add or delete a few. Other requests were mandatory: Some entailed excising a stanza or several lines, representing a significant change in the poem, and others involved major changes (either because the editor wanted me to add or delete a theme or a scene or asked me to revise formal poems whose rhyme scheme and meter already were set). Their offers were as final as their edits: If I didn't revise accordingly, I couldn't resubmit the poems.

Let's take each case and analyze what my options were so that you can make choices to revise or not to revise when you receive similiar requests.

1. *Minor Revisions*
When an editor asks you to change a word or two, or delete a line, or change a title, typically he or she is going to accept the poem with small changes or will even tell you beforehand that the final edit is up to you.

For instance, when poetry editor George Looney considered my poem "The Visit" for publication in *Mid-American Review,* he asked that I change my original title—"Break-In, Discovery: The Visit"—to "Break-In" or "The Visit" and that I drop an epigraph from Freud, which, he said, did not enhance the work. While Looney did not send me a contract when he made the above suggestions, I knew that if I agreed to them, he would. I did, and he took the poem. Case closed.

A few months after I had sold "The Visit" to Looney, I received this letter of acceptance from Jim Schley, an editor in the 1980s at *New England Review and Bread Loaf Quarterly:*

> Dear MJB—
>
> You will be pleased, I'm certain, to hear that we'd like to take "Mary's Heaven." It's very, very beautiful, and utterly haunting. . . .

I am passing on a couple more questions. See these as requests for you to fiddle a little—but *not* as conditions on our acceptance. In line 2, we're a bit confused by the inclusion of "babies still in the womb," since it's not clear what's wrong enough with these babies to propel them into damnation. In the next stanza, I felt that "wraps like a serpent" was too obvious a phrase, especially since the *verb* could do more work and a simile be thereby avoided. I understand the relation or association to the serpent, but feel it's overstated. Similes are like that. Finally, we wonder about the phrase "unbearable pain" which seems ready-made.

In any case, our warmest thanks—

Jim

Even though "Mary's Heaven" had been accepted, I appreciated Jim Schley's comments. Though I kept the phrase "unbearable pain," I fiddled with the line—"babies still in the womb"—because Schley was not sensing the allusion ("still" as in "stillborn"); so I changed it to: "babies lost in the womb." His remark about the simile also was on target. So I deleted "wraps like a serpent" from the lines—"the cord wraps like a serpent/ around the throat..."—and changed it to: "the cord slithers/ around the throat." Schley's suggestions were helpful, but I did them as well because when my name appeared in this prestigious journal, I wanted to present my best possible work.

Finally, Robert W. Lewis, editor of *North Dakota Quarterly,* accepted one of my poems but suggested some minor revisions and even made a few himself. Here is his letter:

Dear Michael Bugeja:

Thank you for your poems. We accept and will publish "Dead or Alive," but we ask you to consider the following points that might result in making a good poem even better.

1. "feels/a need to stall" in stanza 2 is a little weak, a little prolix.

2. "the limo reminding him of a wake" in stanza 3 is also not as tight as it might be and is perhaps too dependent on the rhyme word having to be set up by "reminding him."

3. The last 3 lines of stanza 3: ". . . out of town, wants a county map, a full tank, and a Pepsi.
Nervous, Father offers the goods for free."

4. The two middle lines of stanza 4: "The Man rolls down his window: 'You know/ Who I am?' Father nods, asks him to pay."

These last two suggestions might make the lines sound more idiomatic, more colloquial, to hide the form as it were and to make the father more credible, more tentative.

In any case, let us know your wishes.

Best wishes,
Robert W. Lewis

I did the revisions (see Illustration No. 1 at the end of this chapter). I agreed with the critique. But I would have done the changes anyway because I wanted to work again with Robert W. Lewis. I knew that doing optional edits enhances the poet-editor relationship. Moreover, even if I disliked his suggestions, I also knew that I could always restore the original version of a poem in a future chapbook or book.

Minor edits are just that, too: *minor*. Make them, and you make a new business associate in the process.

2. *Excisions*

These can be painful. When an editor suggests eliminating a stanza, usually you will have to sacrifice a few of your favorite metaphors or images. This was the case with my poems "The Adoption Story" and "Dying, He Curses The Comet" (see Illustrations Nos. 2-3 at the end of this chapter).

In both poems, the excisions were mandatory. In the former, the editor of *The Atavist* wanted me to eliminate the opening stanza; in the latter, the editor of *Poet Lore* wanted me to eliminate the ending lines.

When this happens to you, your first impulse is to say "no." After all, the implication is that your opening or ending was extraneous when you thought that one or the other was crucial in foreboding or resolving the conflct in a particular poem.

Take a breath. Resist the urge to negotiate with an editor, offering to rewrite a few lines or tighten ones in the offending stanza and asking him or her to reconsider the work. You'll be implying that the editor's suggestion was wrong-headed, and that may not go over well.

Of course, you don't have to agree to excise a stanza or lines. If the poem in its current form is that important to you, submit it elsewhere. But keep in mind that an acceptance is at stake and, once again, that you can always restore the original version in a future chapbook or book.

In the case of "The Adoption Story" and "Dying, He Curses The Comet," I agreed to the mandatory excisions. Then I restored the original versions of these poems in my books *The Visionary* and *What We Do For Music*. While the deletions in question may have improved both poems, the restored stanzas and lines enhanced themes of the books in which they appeared. Because I knew my options from the start, the decisions were easy to make.

Other decisions and options, however, can be more complicated.

3. *Major Revisions*

Usually when an editor suggests major changes in a poem and offers the chance to resubmit, I take into account these factors:

- *How badly do I want to place the poem?* Perhaps it has made the rounds for years without a nibble from an editor, and now I have to take a chance and commit to a total overhaul.

- *How badly do I want a byline in a specific magazine?* It is one thing to decline an offer to resubmit a poem to a little magazine and quite another to do the same at *Poetry*.

- *How much work is going to be involved?* Sometimes the time and effort it will take to do major revisions could be used more wisely composing new work.

- *Do I have the ability to execute the suggested changes?* A request may seem to exceed your skill at the moment or, simply, appear impossible to accomplish without totally rewriting the work. (More on this later.)

Only you can address these questions. Certainly, I have declined offers to resubmit poems involving major revisions. For instance, I submitted a four-page poem titled "After Oz," and an editor asked me to rewrite my narrative as a fiction and resubmit it. Nope. Another editor, perhaps not realizing that I had submitted a villanelle, asked me to revise lines so that "they don't repeat themselves." Nope. And a few editors have asked me to rejigger entire poems entailing so much work, with so little indication of an acceptance in their letters, that I decided outright that revising a work wasn't worth my time and effort.

But when Reginald Gibbons, editor of *TriQuarterly,* asked me to resubmit my poem "The Entomologist," I jumped at the chance. *TriQuarterly* is a beautiful and prestigious magazine in which I had always wanted my work to appear. But Gibbons was not making it easy for me. In essence, my poem had a sub-plot—the break-up of the entomologist's marriage—which Gibbons thought detracted from the environmental theme running through the piece. If I could excise the subplot, he said, I could submit the work to him for reconsideration.

I sharpened my pencil and went at it. (See Illustration No. 4 at the end of this chapter.) In essence, I knew that even if Gibbons did not take my poem, he would consider it closely and maybe invite me to submit more poems with similar environmental themes. There was opportunity here. In the end, however, he accepted "The Entomologist."

Another type of major revision involves rhymed and metered verse. Because lines in formal poems usually are predetermined, what seems like a minor suggestion on the surface often can entail hours of intricate rewriting. Scenario: You change one line as advised and suddenly realize that your verse no longer rhymes or scans. So you change the rhyme or the meter in other lines, and before you realize it, you have a nearly new poem instead of a revised one in which an editor has expressed interest.

When I sent this sonnet to Mark DeFoe, then editor of *Laurel Review,* I thought that he would either accept or reject it:

Lullaby, With Balloons

Another lonely weekend, and we cannot wait
For you to sleep. We sing lullabies and leave
Balloons above your crib to instigate
Distraction. In the next room we try to love
Without laughing, though you giggle and goad us.
Maybe the heart-shaped Mylar seems funny afloat
Or the ribbon-tails tickle? You make ruckus
Because you are good at it. You shriek a note,
High C at least, whose pitch and treble amaze
Yet do not stop us. We sigh and moan and so
Do you—echolalia—a silly phase
We think that you are going through. Now go
To bed with your balloons and quit the fuss,
You little pill. You won't uncouple us.

Defoe sent me a rewrite request. He disliked the cliche "You little pill" in the last line, missing the allusion I was making to birth control or, simply, dismissing it altogether. He suggested a new ending in which I should "work back to the child as singer." Finally, he didn't go for the multiple rhyme in the ending couplet and requested a slant rhyme so that the child's song would seem "off-key."

My first impulse was to refuse to do the revision. I knew from a previous workshop experience that changing a line in a sonnet could set off a chain reaction, affecting rhyme scheme and involving hours of rewriting. True, "Lullaby With Balloons" was a Shakespearean sonnet (unlike the Petrarchan type that was critiqued in workshop) so that, at worst, only a quatrain would be affected. But a quatrain is almost one third of a sonnet, and the new lines would have to align themselves with the rest of the poem or other lines would need revising as well. Moreover, while I knew I could easily replace the phrase "You little pill," I did not know if I could "work back to the child as singer" and end with a slant rhyme.

But the longer I studied DeFoe's critique, the more sense it made. So I decided to attempt a revision. I began by circling places in the sonnet that needed work. Then I tackled each one, beginning with the most difficult. Lo and behold, the process suddenly seemed easier than I had remembered it in workshop because I was defining problems and focusing intently on them. Eventually, I rewrote the ending:

> Now go
> To bed with your balloons and quit the fuss.
> Your serenade's off-key. But we'll adjust.

Bingo: another acceptance. Thus encouraged, I composed my first pantoum. I sent what I thought was a fine one to many editors who sent back rejections. Then I tried Joe Taylor, then editor of *Swallow's Tale*. At the time I didn't want an editor to overlook the fact that this was, indeed, a pantoum, so I included the word in the title: "Pantoum for My Side of the Family." Taylor knew the pantoum, all right. He wrote back saying that he would accept mine if I would honor the prescribed form, beginning and ending with the same line and making the third line of the first stanza the second line of the last.

Oops. Three thoughts went through my head:

1. Taylor was right. (I had messed up the form.)
2. I couldn't revise it. (The form was fixed.)
3. The poem was doomed. (This explained all the rejections.)

I froze. It is one thing to change a line in free verse, another to do so in a sonnet, and something else entirely to do the same in a pantoum. Changing a line might topple the form, as fragile as a pyramid of stacked cans in the grocery store. But there were other considerations, too. I wanted a credit in *Swallow's Tale*. I wanted to compose a traditional pantoum. And if I didn't attempt to revise my flawed one, I doubted that it would ever see print. So I had at it. (See Illustration No. 5 at the end of this chapter.) As it turned out, I had the skill after all to accomplish the revision in question. Again I was defining problem areas in my poem and focusing my attention in specific places. I learned an important lesson, too, about revising any poem for publication: If you think that you lack the skill to rewrite a work, or that the suggested changes may be too difficult for you to accomplish, don't make that the sole criterion that keeps you from attempting a revision. Instead, follow this five-step process:

1. Determine what, exactly, an editor wants by circling each suggestion in his or her letter. (If an editor's instructions are vague, send him or her a photocopy of the rewrite request, ask for clarification, and enclose an SASE for the response.)

2. List each suggested change on a separate piece of paper and rank order them (according to your ability) from "most difficult" and "difficult" to "moderately difficult" and "easy."

3. Determine where each suggestion applies in your original version (word, line, stanza).

4. Tackle the most difficult change first if you still have doubts that you can execute it.

5. If you can, you can rewrite the poem according to instructions.

In the case of my original pantoum, I thought that changing the order of lines in the first stanza would make the revision impossible to accomplish or would result in an entirely new poem. I was wrong. In fact, when Taylor accepted the poem, he wrote: "Yes, we would be very pleased to publish the revised pantoum—an enjoyable poem and an interesting use of that form. I like especially the closing stanza." Some ten years later Taylor remembered me from the exchange. Now director of Livingston University Press, he recently accepted one of my collections—*Flight from Valhalla*—which contained, as luck would have it, two pantoums.

Revising for publication has many lasting benefits. It is the final phase in the marketing of poems, establishing stronger bonds with editors and usually resulting in stronger poems.

Illustrations

Poet's Guide

Dead or Alive

Even the air wears a disguise, the dust
Swirling candy wrappers in a mini-funnel
Outside the garage, my father scraping rust
Off junked Packards, surprised by the bell
Announcing a customer in midday heat,
More surprised by The Man in the backseat

Of the limousine. He recalls the bulletin
Board in the post office and the news reels
About bank heists, the feds, shootouts, prison
Escapes. He drops his wad of sandpaper, ~~feels~~ kneels/
~~A need to stall. There is a reward~~ To trace in dirt some numbers—
    there's a reward/
To consider, an escape of his own—*Lord,*

My father thinks, *don't I deserve a break?*
He serves The Man, the pump as cold as a gun
In his hand, the limo ~~reminding him of~~ a wake, as black as
The driver, lost, asks the way out of town,
~~Requests a county map, a full tank and Pepsi.~~ Wants a county map,
    a full tank, and a Pepsi/
Nervous, Father ~~offers him~~ the goods for free. gives

The driver sips his drink, questions how
Dad makes a living, giving things away.
The Man rolls down his window: "~~Do you know~~ You know/
Who I am?" Father nods, ~~and~~ asks him to pay.
Their car screeches off, dust settling
On the road, a funnel of dollars swirling.

The Adoption Story

When the order went out by star
Over Bethlehem, there was doubt,
Not so much of birth and delivery
Unto this world of a savior,
Which Mary and Joseph believed,
As over matters far simpler:
Whether the child would love
And take for his own
Such gracefully chosen parents.

I picture this the first clear
Night of winter, so warm in Oklahoma
I can wrap my daughter in wool
To follow the early Christmas
Lights around the block.
She coos at the flickering
Colors that drape nativities.
Baby, she says, and opens her arms
To the lacquered ceramic: *baby.*

She brings me again to the boy
Told his true father was not
A worker of wood, but of wonder,
And how blood in this mission
Meant nothing. Then the temple,
The mother rebuked for her worry,
The husband's saintly silence.
I have considered silence
And the risk of no risk-taking,

Allowing my daughter to be all
Her blood—even now—would believe

Of itself, of my body. The spirit
This season is truth,
And somewhere tonight I fathomed
The need to pray for such grace
As given a carpenter and wife,
To tell my humbler story
And ease my larger doubts.

Dying, He Curses The Comet

Of the fifty things I could have mentioned,
All of them insignificant—how the hospital
Lights glitter in sunset from the freeway,
How the nurse who brings his dinner slips
An extra pat of butter on the tray, or how,
Perhaps, the Tigers will win the pennant
He will never see—I don't know why
I brought up the Comet, blue and dented,
A real bargain. My father, a mechanic, moaned.
Though he had hours to live, he shooed away
His only son as a king shooes away a clown.
I have thought long on this, come to appreciate
The humor: why would a man burning with cancer
Muster what breath lay in him to indict Detroit?
Where else but America would such tragicomedy ⟵ occur?
~~Occur? True, I didn't consult him. I bought,~~
~~And maybe the pain of such oversight was sharper~~
~~Than we realized. Or maybe he feared it was~~
~~The first of many failures I would meet~~
~~Orphan-like in innocence. Who knows?~~
~~At any rate, the car held together~~
~~Out of spite probably, or some kind of grace.~~

The Entomologist

~~He prides himself on memory,~~ He knows now why insects will/
~~Able to eyeball~~ Inherit the earth, your basic/
~~A quarter of 12,000 species~~ Roach as prehistoric as a shark/
~~Of bee, all 65 variations~~
~~Of mole cricket. But not~~

~~40 some minutes of missing~~
~~Time during which his wife~~
~~Packed a bag and left him.~~
~~What happened? What havoc~~
~~Did he wreak upon them now?~~

~~His conscience is clear~~
~~As lab-light, incandescent.~~
~~He wants her more than anything~~
~~On earth, more than the insects~~
~~That will inherit the earth~~

~~Soon enough, your basic roach~~
~~As prehistoric as the shark~~
Asphyxiating in an oil-slick,//
Your basic ant colony/
Overpopulated as any homosapien/

City, with greater overall bio-/
Mass. You have to admire them,//
The compound eyes and antennae,/
Exoskeletons of armour, stylets/
Sharp as ice-pick, enough

Poison/ in a scorpion to halt
The ~~human~~ heart.// So easy

Then to fall in love/ with
Bugs as a boy, memorizing/
Phyla while his parents fought/

On a farm in Pennsylvania.//
He would slip to the flowering/
Meadow with a canning jar/
Whose lid had no holes for air,/
Mini colisuem, the specimens//

He caught, the gladiators:/
~~Roaches, ants, hornets, honeybees,~~ Lady-, water-, and lightningbugs,/
~~Lady-, water-, and lightningbugs,~~ Butter-, horse-, and dragonflies,/
~~Butter-, horse-, and dragonflies,~~ Roaches, hornets, honeybees—//
~~Spiders, centipedes, pupae—~~

Whatever a boy could trap./
He'd shake them up/
And put the jar to his ear/
As if holding a conch//
To hear the ocean, marveling/

At the hum of aerial insects/
As they attacked the hand-/
Held glass, not each other,//
The crawlers on the bottom/
Racing around the perimeter,/

Playing dead. He did this/
Countless times, and never//
Did a slaughter ensue,/
The captives too intent on/
Overcoming a common plight,/

Another reason to praise them//
More than people. Put people/
In an arena with lethal/

Weapons and no hope of escape/
And they butcher each other.//

Insects at least had priorities./
So while his parents fought,/
Their voices rising in crescendo,/
Their marriage hopeless as a jar,//
He became infatuated with/

The esprit de corps of insects/
Suffocating one by one,/
In the air-tight death-chamber.//
When he dumped out the remains,/
He would hold them lovingly/

In his palm, as if reading/
The future, the importance//
Of pinning the object/
Of passion, classifying it,/
Cataloguing its flaws,/

Traits, and mating rituals,//
~~Minutiae of his marriage~~
In clear focus now/
Under the electron scope/
Of his mind, remembering/

How the roach would stir,//
Drop from his palm,/
And cast a sidelong glance/
At him, knowing whose time/
Was almost up, whose world./

Pantoum for My Side of the Family

~~Girl, say "milk." If you can't~~ Already you're too much like me!/
~~Already you're too much like me!~~ You're just being stubborn:/
~~You're just being stubborn:~~ Girl, say "milk." If you can't/
~~say the goddam word.~~ say the goddam word,//

~~Already you're too much like me!~~ you're just being stubborn:/
Stop that gurgling.
Say the goddam word.
I'll give you some if you

stop that gurgling
this instant. Milk tastes good;
I'll give you some if you
repeat the word.

This instant milk tastes good.
You'll get a drink when you learn to
repeat the word,
which isn't all that difficult.

You'll get a drink when you learn to
speak. . . . Upstart, little
Witch—wasn't all that difficult!
Remember what you just said.

Speak up. Start, little
Girl. Say "milk." If you can't
remember what you just said,
~~you're just being stubborn.~~ already you're too much like me./

Guidebook

Neal Bowers On Working With Editors

During my years as the editor of a literary journal, I often got the impression that writers thought of me as their adversary. To them, I was a troll on the bridge to publication, an unavoidable creature they had to defeat or outwit. All the while, I regarded myself as a friend to writers (being a writer myself), and I wanted nothing more than to find poems I liked well enough to publish. Spending most of my time reading manuscripts that I ultimately rejected (about 98 percent of all submissions) didn't give me feelings of power or superiority. Quite the opposite, in fact; it made me weary and sad, which is partly why I decided to get out of the editing business. Looking back, though, I am proud of the seven years I spent trying to be helpful to writers.

My advice to anyone submitting work for editorial consideration is simply this: Never lose sight of the fact that the editor is a human being, someone with feelings just like yours. He likes to be treated with respect and to be told occasionally that he is valued. I think most editors would agree that their editorial judgments, far from being final or definitive, are largely expressions of their singular tastes. A rejection is nothing personal, and an acceptance is certainly no elevation to sainthood. Both things are the result of the editor's good faith attempt to be honest and fair to the writer.

Editors are not always right. Most of us have turned down work, seen it published later in another journal, and then wondered if we made the right decision. Conversely, we sometimes second guess our own selections when browsing through back issues, occasionally shaking our heads in puzzlement. These doubts are the product of speed. Editors have to work more quickly than they would like, so there isn't time to do much reflecting on an individual work. Consequently, each decision is the product of a specific moment and is usually made under pressure as the clock blinks away the minutes of a vanishing context.

Similarly, when editors make specific suggestions for changes in a manuscript, they do so in some haste and may or may not be tendering good advice. The only person who can say whether or not such suggestions are useful and in the best interest of the work is the author. But experience tells me that most authors are so eager to get into print that they will submit to almost any changes. In revising a work for publication, writers shouldn't be afraid to say when they think suggested changes will weaken a work or alter it beyond recognition. Better to search for another editor than to publish a poem you privately consider maimed by the editorial process.

Whether or not they ever exchange letters or phone calls, writers and editors are engaged in a dialogue with one another about what constitutes good poetry. This can and should be a friendly exchange, if both parties regard one another with respect and keep in mind that they are engaged in a mutual enterprise.

R. T. Smith On Working With Editors

Over the years I have received and taken both excellent and wooden advice from editors, but I hope I've learned by now how to distinguish the glib repair suggestions from genuine corrective surgery. I try to remember that my least negotiable responsibility is not to myself nor to any journal, but to the poem, and I have to be certain that the changes improve the linguistic surface and are in concert with the spirit of the poem as I understand it. For this reason, I'm more likely to give serious consideration to suggestions accompanied by explanations. Editors are always snowed under, and any time one emerges from the drift to comment on one of my poems, I'm going to engage in a dialogue and try not to be defensive. Any poem is a field of possibilities, and I think the final result can only be richer for the options I entertain but resist, so even a decision not to take a particular morsel of editorial advice doesn't mean that I don't appreciate it.

Laurel Speer On Revising Poems

Always be willing to work with editors on revising a poem. Always listen and think about his suggestions. Most editors don't have time, interest or capacity to offer more than perfunctory comment. But never change a line of a poem simply because an editor suggests it. If the suggestion doesn't help or harms the poem, always be willing to withdraw it from possible publication rather than accept editorial changes with which you don't agree.

David Citino On Corresponding With Editors

I am a poet and an editor, so I don't understand myself at all. In fact, it sometimes seems to me that half of me is always at war (or at least locked in grim negotiation) with the other half.

Once, as a young poet, I got a letter from the editor of *The Kenyon Review*, expressing interest in a poem I'd submitted to the magazine but suggesting some revisions—rearrangements of a few stanzas and deletion of a line or two. Well, my first reaction was to write back immediately with a heated response which included my unwavering and passionate belief in my own genius and uncompromising commitment to Art. "My Dear Sir," I would write, "This will not do!" The words "How dare you," and "I am outraged" and "Appalled" came to mind. (I said I was young). Well, I cooled down, I'm happy to say, before I actually wrote the letter, and of course I'm so glad I did.

My initial intransigence was the same unthinking response I see in my own students in introductory writing classes: "But this poem is true; I wrote it exactly as it happened. To change a word would be to deny my vision as Artist." There is (there must be) a difference between the experience that generated the poem and the poem itself—a thing of words, after all. (Thus I'm not criticizing your grandmother but rather the poem about your grandmother which you have written.) And a poem, I tell them, is never ever finished (just as a grandmother is never finished).

The poem of mine that *The Kenyon Review* ended up publishing was better than the one I sent them initially. The editor knew my poem better than I did, and I learned much from his detailed and patient attempt to get me to see—to read myself.

Recommended Assignments

All Levels

1. Continue to submit poems. In fact, research new markets if you haven't already. The more poems you have making the rounds the greater the chance that you will receive a rewrite request.

2. When you get a rewrite request, know your options as explained in this chapter and funnel those requests through the five-step process:

- Determine what an editor wants.
- List and rank order suggested changes.
- Identify where they apply in the original.
- Attempt the most difficult change first.
- Decide whether to continue.

3. Keep a file of all correspondence between you and editors and another file for each draft of your poem, so that you can see what lessons you have learned about revising for publication. Write this information in your journal and refer to it each time you receive a rewrite request, so that you keep learning from experience and honing your technical and marketing skills.

Chapter Six

Assembling Chapbooks and Books

As the editor of a poetry series, I see each year far too many col-lections that are not thoughtfully compiled and arranged. Certainly too many poets submit books and even chapbooks before they're ready to be submitted. And, just as a sentence or a line of poetry has its necessary place and structure, each word and sound and bit of sense being colored by its context, so too a poem in a collection can grow or be diminished by arrangement and placement—by the context we give it.

—David Citino

Format Considerations

No COLLECTION OF poetry is accepted on format considera-tions alone, but published ones all have one thing in common: they read like books, evoking mood or telling a story. Editors are quick to spot them, too, because such manuscripts stand out from piles of mediocre others on their desks.

Rejected manuscripts usually share common mistakes. Typically, many submissions do not contain enough poems to constitute a full-length collection or include too many weak ones. Individual poems may entice, but no thematic or narrative thread unifies the work. By knowing how to assemble poetry collections, you can avoid these pitfalls and eventually publish your work.

First, some basics. There are two formats for poetry collections: chapbooks and books. Chapbooks contain about 20 to 25 pages of verse, single spaced, one poem per page. (Technically, any collection with fewer than 48 typewritten pages qualifies as a chapbook.) Full-length collections average between 48 and 80 pages (with most in the 50- to 60-page range). It would seem that the length of a collection is a simple rule to honor, but many poets don't. Books of 30 to 40 pages are as difficult to market as fiction of 200 pages, too long for a novella and too short for a novel.

In terms of content, a chapbook should read like a novella and a full-length collection like a novel. Ideally, a chapbook should inspire the audience to seek out more of a poet's work. A typical chapbook features between 10 and 15 poems, depending on length of individual selections. Because a chapbook is short, each poem therein should startle or impress the reader. A full-length book should satisfy readers to such an extent that they henceforth will follow the poet's career. A typical volume features between 30 and 50 poems, again depending on length of selections. However, because such a collection can have as many as 80 pages, a poet can include a half-dozen or so less accomplished poems as long as they can stand alone as competent and build on a theme or help complete the plot of a complex story.

In a chapbook or book, each poem should play off other poems for effect. Many collections fail because they read like samplers; poems are clumped together in random order, often to meet page-length requirements, and thus cannot compete with manuscripts whose assembly is pre-conceived.

With competition so keen in the poetry world, knowing when to assemble a collection is as critical as how to assemble one. Generally, new poets should not market collections until they are placing poems regularly in small-press or literary magazines. Just as novelists have to prove a demand for their fiction before they attract agents or publishers, poets have to establish a track record, too. In addition, your inventory of unpublished poems should be three times as great as your *published* work so that you can pick and choose when you arrange poems in a chapbook or book. The more poems at your disposal, the greater the odds of your assembling them in a publishable format.

However, even if you are a beginning poet, it is important to know about publishing chapbooks and books. First, you won't become discouraged by marketing substandard collections only to receive an avalanche of rejections that might dampen your muse. Second, you'll be able to set goals to publish collections within a reasonable time-frame, developing your muse along the way. Third, knowing the basic requirements of book publishing can help you generate more poems than you ordinarily would, enlarging the scope of your muse. Let's see how.

Basic Assemblies

There are three basic arrangements for poetry collections:

1. *Lyrical.* The order of poems focuses on one or related subject(s) and theme(s). Readers do not sense the passage of time in lyric poetry but feel the intensity of a moment as the writer investigates topics as concrete as divorce, war, or ballet and themes as abstract as love, joy, or hate. Each work in a lyrical collection blends like pieces of a jigsaw puzzle until the mosaic of emotion is clear. Finally, when read in sequence, such a book should imply a story or convey drama about the human condition.

2. *Narrative.* The order of poems tells a complex story. Readers sense the passage of time in narrative poetry: first this happened, then this, and finally this event. The plot is wide-ranging: how the poet suffered or survived conflict with individuals,

situations, or natural/extra-natural forces. In addition to plot, poems should imply a theme and foreshadow events: how conflict was resolved through insight, faith, or strength, with critical details provided along the way for suspense or enlightenment.

3. *Combinations.* Lyric poems may be included in narrative collections to highlight theme or moments, and narrative verse in lyrical volumes to provide details and motives. Such a book should be predominantly narrative or lyrical—whatever style best suits the poet's talent—with combinations expressing the most powerful story or emotion.

(Note: Another less common combination features dramatic poems told through one persona as in, say, David Citino's *Appassionata Poems* in which a philosophic Catholic Sister gives lectures. This is, essentially, a lyrical book. Another variation involves dramatic poems told through several personae, as in, say, Frederick Feirstein's *Manhattan Carnival* in which characters interact with each other as in a play. This is, essentially, a narrative book. However, both types contain lyric and narrative moments.)

Whatever the mode of expression, it pays to understand which style serves the book in question. Evaluate your inventory and determine what inspires your muse. For instance, do you:

- Generally depict moments (lyrical) or tell stories (narrative) about one or related aspects of your life . . . or both?

- Find an absence of time-passage (lyrical) or a sense of time-element (narrative) or both, depending on individual poems?

- Deal with situations by focusing on emotions (lyrical) or by piecing together incidents without much comment (narrative) or both?

Once you identify the mode, then you can go about assembling the proper collection if your inventory is large enough.

Warehousing Poems

If you lack a sufficient number of quality poems for a chapbook or book, or require more for the type you have in mind, then you should outline a future collection as a novelist outlines chapters. For instance, before I assembled my first poetry book, *What We Do For Music,* I studied an inventory of about 100 poems and discovered that about 30 concerned the power of music to express emotion. Of these, about 20 were published and strong enough for a book with a unified topic and theme. This shouldn't have come as a surprise because I play several instruments. But as a relatively new poet, I had never stopped to consider the content of my muse.

Such is the benefit of a close inspection of your inventory. Often the muse is composing a book for us without our knowing it. In my case, almost all of my music poems were lyrical, so the shape of my evolving collection also was clear. To help the process in the coming months, I focused my muse and outlined potential book verse in my journal. I ended up composing a dozen more music poems that I probably wouldn't have penned if I had allowed my muse to run freely, without a thought about assembling a specific collection. By doing so, I concentrated on my strengths (music poems), set a career goal (a lyrical book), and generated new poems as this journal excerpt and finished work illustrate:

Excerpt:

7-12-84. Poem about how I love to collect instruments
that I never play, hoarding them in the closet as a miser
hoards gold in a pot.

The Music Miser

The silver I shine comes in two denominations:
Flute and piccolo. Otherwise give me nickel,
The buff keys of a clarinet that fog so splendidly

And then glitter back the karats of my grin.
Give me brass, the pipework of sax and trombone,
Chalice of trumpet, and assorted pots of horn,

Cornet to tuba. Give me a china closetful
Of cymbals stacked like Waterford. Utensils?
Tuning forks. A connoisseur of woodwind and wood,

I'm the Picasso of varnish: violins that drip
With purfling, violas and cellos so tiger-striped
They're caged in velvet. I keep a harem

Of mandolins, their bellies aburst, elegant
Necks ringed with abalone, mother-of-pearl.
Then, the ebony and white—spinet to baby grand—

With ivory like contraband tusk. I can't play
A lick, tone-deaf. If you enter my villa,
Keep quiet. I have one rule: don't touch.

Using this method, I eventually was able to assemble two
other collections in narrative and combined modes. In each
case, I would outline and generate enough verse to constitute a
specific type of book and then begin the process of assembly.
That meant eliminating weak poems and arranging remaining
ones in a proper order.

Proper Assembly

Each type of collection requires a different arrangement of
poems. Order of poems will depend, naturally, on individual
works in one's inventory and the chosen mode of expression.
But methods used in the compilation of my books apply to any
work. For instance, in the lyrical collection *What We Do For
Music,* poems were grouped thematically, according to image
and message. Because no time-element or plot was involved, I
didn't have to relate when I first learned music or performed
professionally, ending with the decision to pursue another

career. (That would have been a narrative collection with a weak plot.) Instead, I selected poems that melded in sequence like a slide show. If a poem featured a saxophone with a theme of love, I followed with another poem about a sax with a theme of regret. Then I included another lyric playing off regret, and so on, with the goal of completing the mosaic of emotion without undercutting theme.

The result was a book that conveyed how a person longed to express truth via sound.

If you are assembling a lyrical collection, ask yourself:

- What poems in my inventory are related by content? Image? Theme?

- What arrangement of poems works best, one that groups poems by content, image, or theme or another that melds them like a slide show to generate drama, continuity, or suspense?

- What message is at the root of each poem and how do those messages stack up against the other? Does the final arrangement convey an overall message that represents the entire collection?

For a narrative collection, as in my book *The Visionary* about the loss of a child, I had to include individual works in the right order to tell a complex story with a plot. Time-element was of essence. So I knew when I had to begin the story, with a poem about losing the baby in a hospital. Then I had to take the reader through the stages of grief, relating specific incidents that foreshadowed a climatic scene when grief is confronted and finally overcome.

In any narrative collection, the goal is to assemble poems so that no individual work disrupts the story. For example, I couldn't have included "The Music Miser" poem in *The Visionary* because it would have confused the audience in form and sense. Simply, the lyric would have stood out among narrative poems about parenthood and loss.

On the other hand, I didn't want to restrict my muse. So I included poems about music only when they continued the plot, as in this narrative employing a metaphor of jukebox and jazz:

The Benevolent Machine

It boomed her heartbeat in the birthing room
And traced only one life on a scroll
Underscored by the baby's
Hopeless line. For hours it wrote

That jagged lyric, then stopped.
A jukebox suddenly unstuck,
It piped something like an infant
Heart: *very like one.*

The nurse knew how to figure
Probability. She held out
Her hand as if to celebrate with my wife,
And felt her pulse.

I don't blame the machine's sensors
For redoubling a heart-echo. I don't blame it
For the scroll we should have kept,
A first sympathy card.

The above poem served the book like a chapter in a 40-chapter novel, leading the reader to the next pertinent incident. The result was a collection that focused upon events in sequence, relating a complex story with an implied theme of faith.

If you are putting together a narrative collection, ask yourself:

- What order of poems tells the story in the most powerful or compelling way, without any disruption?
- How do the details, information, or messages of individual poems stack up against each other? Do they foreshadow events so that the sequence reads like a plot?
- Does the final arrangement build to a climatic scene and resolve conflict?

For a collection combining lyric and narrative verse, as in my book *Platonic Love* about the evolution of a romance, the theme *and* the story are critical. To assemble such a book, I used methods described in the previous two categories. For instance, I included only love poems, sometimes linking them by theme or image as in a slide show and other times by plot as in a script. Lyric poems tended to focus on intense moments, probing feelings, and narrative ones on specific incidents building to a climatic scene. At critical points I would insert a lyric poem to stop the love story and pivot the plot.

Case in point: At one juncture in the story, the narrator remembers what seems to him to be an ancient, predestined attraction to a certain woman. This poem was composed in the narrative mode. Then I pivoted the plot and heightened the moment with my lyric "The Art of Amnesia" suggesting *unrequited* attraction:

> It is a start,

> However dim, for when the triplets move
> Leisurely as these, when they weave
> Their web among the trinkets of

> Formality, at least I forget about love.

Now I could follow this lyric with narrative poems about unrequited love, continuing the story with ever-heightening drama. As in all such collections, the narrative element must enhance the plot and the lyrical element must heighten the drama of a story, encompassing all poetic modes.

If you are assembling a similar book, ask yourself:

- Is my collection predominantly narrative or lyrical? Am I making effective use of each type of poem to relate a story or a theme?

- Are lyric poems included at appropriate intervals to heighten the drama of a story or turn the plot in a new direction? Do narrative poems offer details to enhance theme or convey motive?

- Does the mix of poems in final sequence tell a greater story than a narrative collection or convey a greater theme than a lyrical one?

Once you have answered such questions and determined the mode to suit your work, you should prepare a draft of your manuscript.

Preparing The First Draft

Type up or keyboard your first draft in final-draft fashion to acquaint yourself with the format. If you work with a typewriter, use scrap or recycled paper at this point. If you work with a computer, save the paper and create a new file on your disk. In any case, preparing your first draft as if it were your final one allows you to envision your collection as a book and helps you isolate weak spots that need to be revised.

The standard manuscript contains a title, front matter, and other format considerations. Let's consider each element individually, beginning with the title, so that you can type up or keyboard your manuscript one page at a time.

The title of a chapbook or book often is taken from the title of an individual poem. Look through titles of poems in your final arrangement and decide which title best represents the collection. If no individual title serves the purpose, then consider lines, themes, or images from poems. If none intrigue you, dream up an ideal title and either compose a short poem to be included in your final arrangement or simply let the new title stand alone.

Make two title pages, one with your name, address, and telephone number and another with just the title. These are your first and second pages, respectively. Don't number them; they won't count when you paginate. Some presses demand anonymous readings, so your name should not appear anywhere else in the manuscript. (The first title page is kept in the editorial office for future reference.) Editors who do not require anonymous readings will assume that your first title page contains information for the cover. Copyright notice is unnecessary. If a publisher accepts your work, the press will take out a copyright in your name.

Front matter typically includes acknowledgment, dedication, and contents pages, in that sequence, again unnumbered but counted later when you paginate your manuscript. The acknowledgment page lists magazines that have previously published poems included in the collection. Introduce the publications with the line: "Some of these poems have appeared in x x x," listing the names of magazines. (If you have altered published poems in any way since they appeared in the magazines, include the line: "Some of these poems have appeared, in slightly different form, in x x x.") If your poems have won awards, highlight those separately under the paragraph citing names of magazines.

To illustrate, here's the acknowledgements page from my first book:

> Certain of these poems have appeared in the following magazines: *Amelia, Blue Unicorn, Cincinnati Poetry Review, Chariton Review, Colorado-North Review, Denver Quarterly (INTRO 15), The Devil's Millhopper, Greenfield Review, Indiana Review, INTRO 14, Kansas Quarterly, The Kenyon Review, Negative Capability, New Jersey Poetry Journal, New Mexico Humanities Review, North Dakota Quarterly, permafrost, Poet Lore, RE: Artes Liberales, Small Pond, South Dakota Review, Sun Dog, Texas Review, West Branch,* and *Writer's Digest.*
>
> "Missing" and "The Only Morning My Mother Didn't Worship Her Husband," winners of an Academy of American Poets first prizes, originally appeared in *Cimarron Review.*
>
> "The Mandolin," winner of a *Greensboro Review* literary award, originally appeared in that magazine.
>
> "Re-Defining the Blues," winner of a *Negative Capability* literary award, originally appeared in that magazine.
>
> "Irregular Rhythm," winner of a Foothills Art Center first prize,

originally appeared in *Riverstone* and was later reprinted in *Pudding Magazine.*

The dedication can be a separate page or included above the acknowledgments. It should be simple, no longer than a few words or a single line: *For John; For Jane, my reason for writing; For my mother and father; In memory of my parents;* etc. Underscore to signify italics.

Before preparing a contents page, you have to consider the final arrangement of poems again to decide if you want to break groups of them up into sections. A section is a self-contained mini-chapbook (three or four poems) in a chapbook manuscript and a self-contained chapbook (eight to twelve poems) in a full-length manuscript. Each section indicates a complete break in thought or a change in scene, time, or other story element; but when the sections are read in sequence, they convey a better story or imply a greater theme than if the manuscript continued uninterrupted. In essence, a collection with sections is similar to a poem broken into a sequence, or parts, with each part laying off the other and strengthening or unifying the work.

Most chapbooks and some full-length collections are best presented without any break in the order of poems. Some books, however, read more powerfully if groups of poems are divided. Each work will vary, of course, but poets generally divide books into sections when groups of poems:

- Fall naturally into place by message, image, or scene.

- Augment theme or plot.

- Enhance readability.

If you break your book into sections, you can title these as you would a book by repeating an image, line, or individual title of a poem. Or simply call them "Part One," "Part Two," etc. (or even "One," "Two,"; "I.," "II."; "1," "2"). Insert these and return to the contents, estimating how many pages it will require. Then count all pages used for front matter—acknowledgments, dedications, and contents—and number poems accordingly. (The first poem should start with "3" or "4," depending on length of contents.) After you have paginated your manuscript, return again to the contents and add numbers after titles on the same line. To illustrate these concepts, here is the contents page of *What We Do For Music*:

CONTENTS

If you prepare your manuscript as above, you will be able to envision your complete collection. But don't print it up on good bond or send it out yet because you will have to revise.

Preparing The Final Draft

Until a book appears in print, you won't have a real *final* draft. It is typical for poets to revise collections several times before manuscripts are accepted and ultimately published. But for purposes here, a final draft means that the manuscript is ready to be submitted to and reviewed by an editor.

Don't be taken in by your first draft. Refine it at least one more time before you even think about submitting it to a publisher. Sometimes switching the order of a few poems empowers theme or plot. Or perhaps you have composed more verse and want to replace certain poems or add new ones in the collection. So let the manuscript cool for a month and then reread the sequence, making adjustments. Follow these tips:

- Delete weak poems, even ones that further the plot or heighten the moment of a collection. Each poem should stand alone. So revise the poem(s) in question, substitute different poems from your inventory, or create a new work to fill the slot.

- For a lyrical collection, make a copy of the contents page. Read each poem. Consider images and themes and jot them down next to the titles in the margin of the contents page so that you can get a feel for the entire collection. Often you'll discover misplaced poems that could play off each other better if they appeared in different places in the manuscript. If so, rearrange the order so that the lyric mode has greater impact when articulating theme or implying plot.

- For a narrative collection, take the contents page out of the manuscript and study it as if each poem were a chapter in a novel. Now read each poem and write a sentence in your journal describing what happens. Often you'll find scenes out of sequence or gaps between scenes during which readers may lose or become confused with the plot. Sometimes you will find redundancies, two poems—one weak, one strong— describing the same incident. To remedy these problems, rearrange poems, substitute or compose new ones, and delete as needed to make your plot complete.

- For a combined collection of lyrical and narrative verse, make another copy of the contents page. On it, identify which poems are lyric and narrative. With lyric poems, follow the procedure as explained above for lyric collections. With narrative poems, do the same as explained above for narrative collections. Now analyze the "chapters" of your plot as articulated by individial narrative poems. Isolate key moments during which you may want to heighten drama or suspense. Now return to the contents page and determine whether you have a lyric poem at that juncture and, if you do, whether the theme and imagery of that poem contributes to the story line. Make the necessary adjustments by rearranging, substituting, or composing new poems.

After you have assembled a final draft, retype or print it according to standard format. Be sure to change the contents pages to reflect any change in poems or pagination. Use the contents page to check every poem and page number for accuracy.

If you employ methods as explained in this chapter, you will generate more poems if you are a beginning poet. If you are more experienced, you will end up with collections, prepared according to standard format, that read like novellas or novels. In either case, an editor eventually will honor that effort with a close reading because your manuscript will stand out from the typical piles on his or her desk. When final decisions are made, your chapbook or book may rise to the top.

Guidebook

Kelly Cherry On Assembling Books

Once I heard the late William Stafford describe how he went about putting a book manuscript together. Whenever he had written enough poems to make a book, or perhaps more than enough, he spread them out on the floor. Then he picked them up in the right order.

There are poets who live by their own chronology. Putting a book together, they arrange their poems in chronological order. They even date their poems.

Neither of these methods is open to me. I rewrite some poems over a period of years, perhaps decades; in any case, I've never been able to manage even a diary for very long, and keeping track of what I wrote when would make me much too self-conscious.

More than that, I need time to think a thing—anything— through. A poem I wrote last month may suggest an idea I'll return to next year; a poem I wrote this month may suggest a different idea, which I'll return to at a still later time. At some point, I begin to perceive themes, subjects, motifs. A book begins to shape itself around one idea or another; it begins to occur within a specific arena. This poem and that poem, taken together, lead the way to another poem, one I might never have found otherwise, and the manuscript discovers itself. It is as if the book knows what it needs to contain in order to become itself. This book may incorporate poems written at widely varying times. It will have to leave out many poems that don't belong in that book's domain.

But there are other themes, subjects, motifs, other books to be written wherein some of those poems will find a place.

Neal Bowers On Assembling Chapbooks & Books

A good friend of mine once told me he organized his first poetry collection alphabetically, by poem title. When the book was subsequently chosen as the winner in a book competition and published by a reputable press, his cynical view that organization didn't matter seemed confirmed. I've always thought that the contest judges must have sensed in the manuscript some recurrent themes and intuited a coherence that the poet was too jaded to perceive for himself. Sad, really, because framing a manuscript can be an invigorating process for the author, an occasion for discovering things about one's own work.

Most poetry books are collections of individual poems written over a period of years. The challenge for the poet setting about to make a book out of such disparate materials is to perceive his own obsessions. I recommend starting by assembling a stack of all poems written during the most recent four or five year period; then read through the pile, making a spontaneous decision to eliminate some from consideration and to keep others for another look. Typically, the "keeper" pile is much smaller than the pile of rejected poems. The next step is to take this smaller pile and read through it again, looking this time for congruities in subject matter, point of view, tone, and theme. Some poems will readily herd together; others will remain mavericks. Those that can be grouped fairly easily will possibly become individual sections in the collection. Those that can't will either be eliminated from further consideration or else they will drive the poet to produce more work to go with them. In this way, the poet can actually get inspiration from the book organizing process. In the end, the completed manuscript will be between 50 and 70 pages long and will reflect the poet's best effort to perceive the thematic unity of his own work.

Writing a book of poems with an organizing principle in mind is another way to proceed, though it isn't necessarily easier than the method just described. When the theme or central subject is known in advance, the risk of writing prescriptively is increased, and the poet may mechanically produce poems to fill his preconceived pages. The only way to avoid this pitfall is to resist the temptation to plot the book before anything is written. Far better to use the book's organizing idea as a stimulus, and to be flexible enough to allow the poems that come spontaneously to modify the idea, even if they tend to be off the mark of the initial plan.

Full-length collections are much more difficult to organize than chapbooks, simply because they are so much longer. To put things in musical terms, a book is a symphonic production; a chapbook is a tune with only a few variations. Because it is typically only 16 to 32 pages long, the chapbook affords a much more concentrated space, thus allowing the poet to be strongly focused. The best chapbooks, I think, are those that recognize their brevity as an asset and present material that is tonally and thematically unified. There are too few pages for the poet to show all the modulations of his voice, but the space is perfect for a single, compelling song.

Recommended Assignments

Beginning Level

Read your inventory of poems and ascertain whether you would like to write a lyrical, narrative, or combined collection. Study the topics, themes, and stories of poems in your inventory and ascertain as well if you are already writing a specific book. If so, in a journal or notebook, outline more poems related to your favored topic, theme, story, and compose them at your leisure until you have a chapbook or book. If not, study the topics, themes, and stories of your *best* poems and consider basing a chapbook or book on them. Then, in your journal or notebook, outline new poems and compose them until you have such a collection.

Intermediate Level

Do the Beginning Level exercise again to determine whether the poems in your inventory are suggesting another chapbook or book. If so, outline ideas for more poems related to your new favored topic, theme, or story. At this point, you should have enough final drafts of poems in your inventory to assemble a chapbook. Prepare one according to steps outlined in this chapter. If you feel you have enough poems for a full-length collection, try your hand at that as well.

Advanced Level

By now, you should have enough final drafts of poems in

your inventory to put together a full-length collection. Do so according to steps outlined in this chapter.

Additional Exercises For All Levels

Visit the library and check out a dozen new collections by contemporary poets. Try to pick books by different presses. Analyze the mode—lyrical, narrative, combined?—and study the arrangements of poems. Make observations in your journal. Ascertain editorial preferences of individual presses and use this information for marketing purposes later.

Chapter Seven

Placing Chapbooks
and Books

It's too easy for fairly well-published poets to say, as I'm about to say, that publication shouldn't be the major goal for young poets. But I do think, along with Donald Hall and many others who've spoken on this subject, that there's too much of a rush into print for many people still in their poetically formative years. I was guilty of publishing poems long before they were ready, and I seriously regret having done so. I'm more patient these days, and thankful to be. There's one whole book (not, happily, one of my Louisiana State University books, but an earlier one, at long last out of print) that needed about five more years of gestation; instead, it was born underdeveloped, weak and pallid. I feel a tiny bit guilty for not loving it, and for being embarrassed by it.

—Susan Ludvigson

Chapbook And Book Publishing Options

COLLECTIONS OF POEMS are difficult to market because of these factors:

1. Although readers of poetry are dedicated and often follow the careers of poets by purchasing each of their books, the over-

all audience is relatively small; so small, in fact, that many major newspapers refuse to review collections, earmarking space instead for non-fiction and fiction books.

2. Although a record number of poets are composing today and comprising a large part of the audience, many do not buy poetry collections and so do not support the market in which they hope one day to succeed.

3. Although hundreds upon hundreds of collections are published each year, thousands upon thousands of poets keep composing them, adding to the incredible surplus cluttering editors' desks.

Those are the market conditions, but you can overcome them. Begin by submitting a chapbook instead of a full-blown collection. Production costs for chapbooks are significantly lower, of course, increasing the odds that an editor will invest time and money in the work of a relatively unknown writer. After you have published a chapbook or two, you may want to market a book-length volume. Editors are interested in poets who have publishing experience and an audience already following their work. So if you research the market and target the right editor with a quality manuscript, you stand a good chance of placing a major collection.

Here are your publishing options:

1. *Standard Publishing.* A commercial, literary, or small-press publisher considers submissions and/or conducts competitions.

Commercial presses like Random House or Norton publish mostly best-selling novels and non-fiction books, adding a poetry collection or two to the roster for prestige.

Literary presses are often located in universities and typically consider manuscripts only one or two months per year, often conducting competitions that require you to send a reading fee. But because profit-motive often is not the chief concern, and because designers and printing presses are on staff or in-house, literary publishers usually produce magnificent-looking books with high prestige.

Small presses are owned by private individuals whose reading cycles and products vary according to how much time and money the persons have invested in their enterprises. Some consider manuscripts all year and others, only one month per year. Some require reading fees, some do not. By far, however, the small press is responsible for most chapbooks being published today and may be your best bet if trying to break into the market. Also, many editors own printing presses or computer systems to publish collections, and take pride in their product— from type font to paper stock. Thus, a small press book can be as attractive as a commercial or literary one.

If your work is chosen under standard contract by a commercial, literary or small press, the publisher pays all production costs and you get 10 percent royalties on the wholesale or retail price. Sometimes you get no royalties until your book turns a profit; then you get your 10 percent. Occasionally, you get no royalties whatsoever but receive 10 percent of the press run. Publishing chapbooks and books under a standard contract is the goal (and dream) of most poets.

2. *Cooperative Publishing.* The poet works with the publisher in some capacity and shares the burdens of publication.

Because of the declining market for poetry and the increasing costs of production, a few smaller commercial publishers and many small presses require the poet to bear some of the risk involved in publishing a work. Also, many writers' groups engage in the cooperative option to give members a chance at publishing chabooks and books and to increase the market for poetry in general.

Arrangements vary, so be on your guard. Make sure you can fulfill your end of the bargain before signing agreements. Some cooperative agreements require the poet to pay certain costs of production. Others require the poet to participate in the printing or marketing phases of production. A few require the poet to contribute money in a fund for books by other poets, put in hours typesetting or operating a press, and/or doing promotions to market the house's various collections. In any case, cooperative publishing is highly respected by the literary establishment, and you should look into it if you cannot place your collections with publishers offering standard contracts.

3. *Self-publishing.* The poet publishes his or her chapbook or book, engaging and paying for services by typesetters and printers or doing part or all of the production work alone.

True, many good poets have self-published. Also many impatient ones. The practice may be respected in the literary world but the product usually is overlooked (especially by book reviewers). If you are just starting out, self-publish your work only if you are not interested in making a name for yourself in poetry but simply want to share your verse with friends, colleagues, and loved ones. On the other hand, if you have been publishing for years and dislike marketing or cannot place your book manuscripts, you may want to self-publish a work now and then because you probably have a following already and should be able to recoup your investments. If you decide to self-publish, typically you'll work with local printers, invent a name for your "press," publish your book, own all copies, advertise to sell them, and collect all proceeds. But mostly you will foot the bill, so schedule modest press runs of 100 to 300 copies (or a maximum 500 if you have a following).

Also look into cheaper ways to make books, especially if you own or have access to a computer with design programs. Design pages on the screen, print out typeset galleys, assemble the book, and take it to a photocopying center. Representatives there will help you choose a cover and explain ways to bind your book. You can save hundreds of dollars. Before you decide to self-publish, check out *The Complete Guide To Self-Publishing* by Tom and Marilyn Ross (Writer's Digest Books).

4. *Vanity/Subsidy Presses.* A subsidy company guarantees acceptance of your manuscript, and you pay all costs.

Few editors and fellow poets respect subsidy publishing. You won't sell many of your books to libraries, either, because shelf space is too tight to stock such books. Promotion is difficult, too. Under such arrangements, advertisements for a book usually are collective—20 books getting one blurb line apiece—and placed in the general media (rather than in specific outlets: i.e. small-press and literary magazines). Sometimes you own all copies, sometimes you own only part of the press run. Some agreements are less predatory than others, but all bank on your general ignorance of publishing and willingness to pay handsomely to see your byline on a book.

Nonetheless, many subsidy presses put out magnificent-looking collections for thousands of dollars (out of your pocket). So consider this: It costs about the same amount of money under the typical vanity contract as it does to self-publish a chapbook per year for a decade or to buy a used printing press or high-tech computer equipment. Do the latter, become a reputable publisher yourself, and expand the market for poetry.

Marketing Strategies

Poets with collections who are seeking to publish via standard contracts need to know marketing strategies if they hope to place their verse. Competition is keen. The typical publisher accepts one or two books per year (with a press run of 500 to 1,000) and receives about a thousand manuscripts in a 30-day reading cycle.

To increase your odds:

1. *Avoid the big-time commercial press.* Companies in this category are household names because of their best-selling novels and non-fiction books. Don't bother submitting to them, at least early on in your career.

To test the waters, once I sent sample poems and letters of inquiry to 10 Madison Avenue publishing houses, noting that I had received major fellowships and had published three full-length poetry books and more than three hundred individual poems in magazines. Two houses didn't bother to reply. Only one house read and responded to the poems. This standard rejection from Random House was typical of what I received:

Thank you for your recent letter. I am sorry to report that Random House publishes very little poetry, and the small amount we do take on is usually the work of well known poets. May I suggest that you try submitting your work to smaller publishing houses and to periodicals?

Big-time commercial publishers often employ well-known poets as outside readers. They are hired because of their expertise and are similar to baseball scouts looking for talent in the minor leagues. They know what they want, and they want whom they know. Sometimes in-house editors of these publishing companies accept the work of successful novelists already on their lists. The editors do this in part as a favor to the novelist, but they also realize that the novelist already has a mass following and because of that, his or her book will be reviewed and easily could sell out a modest press run.

2. *Identify presses.* In order to market poetry collections, you have to identify publishers who seek such manuscripts. Use basic directories like *Poet's Market* to get a sense of literary style and editorial content of the individual presses. If you have a chapbook numbering 20-25 pages, look for presses specializing in that format; if you have a full-length collection numbering 48-80 pages, identify those. In either case your best chance will be with small-press and university houses that stress objective readings and/or sponsor annual contests.

Jot down at least three dozen publishers for each chapbook or book that you wish to market. As you research each press, you'll eventually want to narrow that list to the best twelve. With that many outlets, you will have a shot at publishing your work.

3. *Research presses.* Before you invest the time and money involved in photocopying, querying, and marketing a collection, you should investigate the needs of specific publishers. Under typical entries in directories you'll find the names of poets previously published by the press. Crosscheck these names in reference books found in the typical library. Such books include directories that list the books and biographies of con-

temporary poets or that cite poets' publications in magazines, journals, and respected anthologies. It's a plus if a name appears in these reference books, indicating that the house publishes experienced poets with whom you may want your work to be associated.

Record the names of these poets in your journal and determine if your library has their books. (If not, many libraries can get such books through various loan systems with other libraries.) If you can find an author's name, address and telephone number in *A Directory of American Poets and Fiction Writers* (Poets & Writers), you often will be able to contact the poet directly and ask if he or she was pleased with the press in question and the production/distribution of the chapbook or book.

At the very least, check out the collections or send away for sample copies. When you get the books, you should be able to evaluate the quality of production and the style and genre of verse. Some publications will be nothing more than photocopied pages stapled with card or matte covers, an inexpensive format that may not appeal to you. Or the style and genre of verse may be the opposite of your own, featuring experimental when you compose formal poems (or vice versa).

In any case, before you submit a manuscript, you should have an idea of how your book will look and what the editor's tastes may be. Otherwise, you will be taking a hit-and-miss approach, wasting supplies, postage, time, and energy. Worse, you can place a good collection with an amateur publisher whose product may embarrass or disappoint you.

4. *Request guidelines.* Once you have identified suitable presses for your work, you need to request guidelines to know when and how to submit your manuscripts.

To request guidelines, write a brief business letter and include an SASE. Typical guidelines spell out page-length requirements, reading cycles and fees, and other pertinent data that must be followed to the letter.

Keep a file of these guidelines as a future marketing tool. You also may want to make notations based on your research about each press, the quality of its publications, and its editorial tastes. Staple or clip these notes to the guidelines and you will have a complete, personalized directory of presses.

5. *Submit manuscripts.* Keep a log as you learned how to do in the chapter on marketing poems, identifying where a manuscript has been sent, how long it has been out, and when it was rejected or accepted.

Although editors of magazines dislike simultaneous submissions, publishers of chapbooks and books usually encourage them because your chances of winning a contract are so slim. Also, if you're paying a reading fee, you should have the right to submit elsewhere. Consequently, when you have found a dozen potential markets, submit your chapbook or book to all of them during the requisite reading cycles. If your work is accepted elsewhere, notify other editors immediately. Most will appreciate your professionalism and will be glad to consider your next volume. If your work is rejected by your dozen select markets, search for new ones or try old ones again. (Many presses feature different judges each year, so submit to them in the next reading cycle.)

To submit a manuscript, refer to your sets of guidelines. Typically, guidelines will tell you a history about the press, define eligibility requirements, and state contest rules and typing formats. (Most presses consider manuscripts with single- or double-spacing, but a few prefer one or the other so you may want to have originals in both formats.) Many presses prefer that you do not list your name anywhere else but on the first title page. A few want your name and/or address on all pages. (If submitting to the latter press, *pencil* your name and address on each page of a photocopy so that you do not waste time typing or printing out a new original.)

Here is a typical set of guidelines from *Pearl,* a magazine that sponsors an annual chapbook competition:

GUIDELINES FOR PEARL'S
ANNUAL CHAPBOOK CONTEST

MANUSCRIPTS should be *unbound* and include: a title page with the author's name and phone number; an acknowledgment page listing previously published poems; 20-24 pages of poetry; and an SASE for return of manuscript. Manuscripts should be typed, pages numbered, and **name should appear on title page only.** *Clear* photocopies and *letter-quality* computer print-outs are acceptable.

$10 ENTRY FEE includes a copy of the winning chapbook. All other proceeds go to the continuing publication of *Pearl.*

SASE: If you prefer your manuscript not be returned, please enclose a 6"x 9" self-addressed envelope and 75 cents postage for receipt of the chapbook.

JUDGING: Each year's contest is judged by an established poet, who will be announced just prior to the submission period. (Past judges have included Gerald Locklin, Laurel Speer, and Robert Peters.) The selection of manuscripts for final judging will be made by the editors of *Pearl.* All entires are read anonymously.

SUBMISSION PERIOD: Manuscripts are accepted each year from May 1 through July 1. The winner is announced and manuscripts returned by mid-November.

PRIZE: The winner will receive $100, publication, 50 copies, and an introduction by the judge of that year's contest.

* Last year's winning chapbook is available for $5, post-paid.

Note: do not base submissions on these guidelines, subject to change.

Book guidelines, similar to those for chapbooks, typically have stricter rules governing eligibilty. For instance, some presses only publish first books. Some are interested only in the work of poets who already have published a full-length book. Still others stipulate age restrictions, some soliciting work from younger poets (under 40) and others from older ones (over 40). Some presses restrict the number of manuscripts that can be sent by the same poet during one reading cycle. Here are eligibility restrictions (subject to change) from Anhinga Press guidelines:

> The Anhinga Prize is open to poets who have not previously published more than one full-length (over 48 pages) book of poetry. Poems previously in journals and anthologies may be included in the manuscript, provided the poet has retained copyright and notifies Anhinga Press of the publications.

> Authors may submit as many manuscripts as they wish, as long as all submissions conform to these rules. Manuscripts submitted in previous years and manuscripts under consideration by other publishers are eligible.

Presses that do not solicit book-length manuscripts via competitions increasingly are requiring poets to send samples of their work rather than complete manuscripts. Again, guidelines will inform you about specific policies, saving you time and money. If the guidelines ask you to "query with a sample of your work," write a detailed cover letter describing the type of collection (length, topic, theme, style: narrative, lyric, or combined); your publishing history (number of poems placed in magazines); and your background (job, hobbies, etc.). Also, you might let the publisher know how you will participate in the promotion of your collection (i.e., doing local readings, identifying potential reviewers, or helping to sell your book to people who know you.) Write the letter in standard business style and keep it to one single-spaced page. Then include your best poems —or a sequence of poems—that represent the collection. (Typically, a sample totals between 10 and 15 pages of poetry for a full-length book.) If the editor is interested, you will be invited to submit the complete collection.

Now you have to wait for the verdict. Typically, if your manuscript is accepted, you will receive a telephone call from the publisher conveying the good news. Otherwise, you'll have to depend on the mail.

If you have entered a chapbook or book competition, the editor will send you results. If you are a finalist or semi-finalist, you earned a high honor and should list that in cover letters to other presses when you resubmit your manuscript. If you have sent your work to a publisher who has solicited the entire manuscript, you will receive a standard rejection, a personal note ("thank you" or "this came close"), or a formal letter of rejection. If you receive a formal letter addressed to you (rather than to "Contestant" or "Poet") and the letter praises specific poems (distinguishing it from a *form* letter), the editor appreciated your manuscript and considered accepting it. He or she may give you the opportunity to try again (with or without revision). Take it. Moreover, if you are coming close to publishing your chapbook or book, or becoming interested in cooperative publishing, you should know how to promote your work. That knowledge alone can help you negotiate with an interested editor to close a deal.

Promoting Your Book

Case study: In 1990, I sent a book manuscript to Roger Lathbury at Orchises Press. He read the submission carefully and wrote me a formal rejection letter, praising the work but ultimately deciding against publication. Here is an excerpt from his letter:

> Thank you for letting me look at *The Visionary,* which arrived ten days ago. I read through it last and then this weekend with pleasure, enjoying the dark, lonely complexity of family that I see as its main focus and watching it move with or against—I couldn't always tell which—the ecclesiastical framework you've given the collection. This is rare: most collections come to me unshaped or unformed by any larger unifying frame.

And yet, as a whole, not enough of these poems feel right to me so that I'd be comfortable publishing this collection. . . . I am pleased to have been given the chance to see *The Visionary* and regret that it was so close then no go.

I was pleased that the publisher had taken the time to read my work carefully and made a point to send another manuscript to him as soon as I had completed one. In the interim, *The Visionary* was accepted by another publisher in England. When I had a new collection, I submitted it to Roger Lathbury and, a few months later, received another formal rejection letter that praised the new work even more than *The Visionary*. Lathbury wrote: "I liked much of *Platonic Love,* but don't want to take it now, if indeed I should do it at all." He added that perhaps I should try a larger publishing house. If I had no luck in a year or so, he advised, I could resubmit the book to Orchises.

At this point, I decided to telephone Lathbury. I could have written him but thought that I could close the deal in a discussion, especially if I offered to take an active role in promoting the book. Lathbury was interested in what I had to say, but wondered if I could help with typesetting and design, since I knew both as a working journalist. In a small sense, then, this would be a cooperative venture. I agreed, and he accepted. It was the beginning of a good partnership. When *Platonic Love* was so successful that Lathbury made a tidy profit, he invested it in another collection, *After Oz,* and later agreed to do an American reprint of *The Visionary*—the book that started it all.

I learned much about negotiating contracts from my Orchises experience. Recently, a publisher sent me a reluctant letter of rejection for a collection of essays; so I telephoned her and offered to help market and promote the book. She accepted my offer, and I closed another deal. Here's how you can, too:

- *Offer to compile mailing lists.* A mailing list is a compilation of names and addresses of friends, colleagues, family members, librarians, book reviewers, and acquaintances who may be interested in your work. You want to compile at least 100 names; between 250 and 500 names is ideal. (You'll be surprised at how many people who know—from former classmates and teachers to ex-employers and colleagues.) The publisher will contact them with a flier, card, or catalogue describing your book. Typically, only 10 percent of your list will order your collection, but that may be enough to persuade an editor to invest in your work.

- *Arrange book signings.* Contact managers of area bookshops to see if they would be willing to host author's parties should your collection be accepted for publication. Do the same with area librarians. (Even try a few arts & crafts shops.) If possible, ask them to put these offers in writing and make copies of these letters, sending or mentioning them to editors when you are closing a deal.

- *Offer to schedule readings.* Publishers usually are eager to work with poets who do readings because listeners may buy books at such events. If you are negotiating with an editor, explain that you will plan a series of readings when your work is published, to promote it.

Of course, these methods also apply to promoting and marketing chapbooks and books that have won contests or that have been accepted via standard contracts. You won't be closing a deal in such a case, but you *will* be impressing editors who may want to see future collections because they appreciate the fact that you take such an active role in the publishing process. Unlike many others, you'll know how to sharpen your verse in a workshop, perform readings, enter contests, market poems and, ultimately, assemble and sell them. When you do, you'll reach more than a pinnacle in your career. You'll reach an audience.

Guidebook

Leonard Trawick On Editorial Preferences

It is common sense to check out some of the books from a potential publisher before submitting, to make sure that they are interested in your kind of poem. Is there an old-boy or old-girl network that favors poets personally acquainted with the editors? Undoubtedly some of this goes on. Any editor who knows you is likely to read your manuscript with more care, so there is no reason to go out of your way to avoid meeting a potential publisher. But I think quality eventually rises to the top. In fact, the Cleveland State University editorial committee seems to bend over backward to avoid favoritism, so that, of the more than ninety poets we have published, I have known very few before we accepted their manuscripts.

I can only repeat the common advice not to try to sell the manuscript in a cover letter. I am immediately put off as soon as a poet begins to explain the book and tell me how great it is, or worse, how great he or she is. On the other hand, I am impressed by a substantial acknowledgments page: if six or eight good magazines have liked some of these poems, they are probably worth my attention. Getting individual poems published is an important step toward getting the book accepted.

Ron Wallace On Revising Accepted Books

Faced with the burden of judging hundreds, or thousands, of book-length submissions annually, few poetry editors these days routinely help poets revise their books as they did in an earlier era. The book that is ultimately accepted must thus be more than promising; it must be virtually perfect.

But even the book good enough to survive the rigorous competition can benefit from a dedicated editor's eye. I've been very lucky in having such an editor in Ed Ochester at the University of Pittsburgh Press. Ochester, and any really good editor, I would suggest, clarifies weaknesses in a work which the author, at some level, has probably already suspected, but has repressed or refused to acknowledge.

I don't remember who said that all great works are collaborations, but it's probably true, and although I rarely show my book manuscripts to anyone but the obligatory editor before they're published (a self-protective practice I recommend to no one), I am grateful to Ed and others for prodding me to strengthen my books (by suggesting additions and deletions and restructurings) and my individual poems (where a change as small as a word or a comma can prevent an unintentional pratfall).

It is always difficult to reopen the case of a poem you thought was closed, but it may be ultimately necessary to save an innocent victim.

Recommended Assignments

Beginning Level

Even though you may not have a chapbook or book for submission, study marketing procedures as explained in this chapter and identify and research presses, request guidelines, and create a file of potential markets for your work.

Intermediate Level

1. Assemble a new chapbook.

2. Update and expand the Beginning Level exercise. Identify presses that publish work similar to your own. Follow guidelines, study sample copies of books, and then send your chapbook out in a simultaneous submission to a dozen presses.

3. While you are awaiting word, prepare a mailing list.

Advanced Level

1. Assemble a new full-length collection.

2. Update and expand your marketing file and mailing list. Then send your book manuscript to at least six presses in a simultaneous submission.

3. Contact publishers who express interest in your work and offer to promote or otherwise help produce the book, to close the deal.

APPENDIX

Glossary

Acknowledgments: A list of poems and the magazines in which they were first published, usually included at the beginning or end of a chapbook or book. (Also known as "acknowledgements page.")

Bio note: A brief description, usually no longer than 50 words, of a poet's publications, job, hobbies, or lifestyle, etc.

Contributor's note: Same as "bio note."

Contributor's copy: Free copy of a magazine in which your poem(s) appears.

Credit(s): Publication(s) in a magazine.

Directory: Compilation of freelance markets or authors, citing such information as names, addresses, and telephone numbers.

Entry: A poem, manuscript of poems, chapbook or book sent to a contest in the manner described in the guidelines.

Entry fee: Small amount of money, usually $5-25, which an author must pay for his or her entry or manuscript to be considered in a contest or by a publisher. (Also known as "reading fee.")

Galley: Typeset poems sent from a publisher to a writer so he or she can check the copy for errors, omissions, and typos.

Guidelines: Proper procedures, described in a handout or flier, that an author must follow when making a submission to a magazine, publisher, or contest.

Log: A list of poems, the dates and places to which they were sent, and the decision (acceptance, rejection, rewrite request).

Manuscript: Usually 3-5 poems. (The term, abbreviated "ms" or "mss" in the plural, also refers to an unpublished chapbook or book.)

Multiple submission: Sending more than one manuscript to a magazine before its editor has decided on previously sent submissions.

Periodical: A magazine.

Poetry symbols: One slash at the end of a line, illustrated thusly— / —means "line break," or the place the line stops; two slashes— // —means "stanza break," or the place the stanza stops.

Proofs: Same as galley.

Query: A letter in which the poet asks an editor a) if he or she would like to consider a manuscript or b) is able to report on the status of a manuscript.

Reader: A person at a magazine or a contest judge or screener who evaluates manuscripts.

Sample copy: An issue of a magazine or an edition of a chapbook or book that a freelance poet solicits from an editor or publisher (usually paying for the product and providing return postage) so that he or she can study and analyze it for marketing purposes.

SASE: Self-addressed stamped envelope.

Sequence: A series of poems in a chapbook or book.

Simultaneous submission: Sending the same manuscript to two or more magazines or publishers.

Status: The progress of a manuscript through the marketing process: lost in the mail, lost in the office, rejected, still under consideration, rewrite request forthcoming, accepted for publication.

Submission: A manuscript of poems or a chapbook or book sent to a magazine or publisher with adequate return postage and a self-addressed envelope.

Vanity press: A publisher who accepts work regardless of its merit and requires the author to pay a significant portion of production costs to see the poem, chapbook, or book in print.

Index

About the Author

MICHAEL J. BUGEJA, 43, is a writer and poet with some 500-plus credits in literary magazines, including *Harper's*, *Poetry*, *The Georgia Review*, *The Kenyon Review*, *New England Review*, *Prairie Schooner*, *TriQuarterly*, *Quarterly West*, *The Formalist*, *Hellas*, *Indiana Review*, *Graham House Review*, and *Antioch Review*. His writing has been anthologized in *Contemporary Literary Criticism* and *Anthology of Magazine Verse & Yearbook of American Poetry*, among others.

He has six book-length collections of poems: *Talk*, University of Arkansas Press, forthcoming; *Flight from Valhalla*, Livingston University Press, 1994, (nominated for the Pulitzer Prize); *Platonic Love* and *After Oz*, Orchises Press, 1991 and 1993; *What We Do For Music*, Amelia Press, 1990; *The Visionary*, Taxus Press, England, 1990 (reprinted by Orchises Press in 1995). In addition, he has written two books of social criticism: *Culture's Sleeping Beauty: Essays on Poetry, Prejudice, and Belief* (Troy, N.Y.: Whitston, 1992) and *Academic Socialism: Merit and Morale in Higher Education* (Orchises, 1994). He also has published two poetry texts, *The Art and Craft of Poetry* (Writer's Digest Books, 1994) and *Poet's Guide* (Story Line Press, 1995). A journalism textbook, *Living Ethics: Developing Values in Mass Communication*, was published in 1995 by Allyn & Bacon/ Paramount. A collection of award-winning short stories published in America and Europe and titled *Little Dragons* is forthcoming from Negative Capability Press.

Bugeja's writing awards include a National Endowment for the Arts fellowship, fiction; a National Endowment for the Humanities grant, culture; an Associated Writing Programs anniversary award, poetry; an Academy of American Poets award; *Writer's Digest* Grand Prize, fiction; The Strousse Award, poetry, *Prairie Schooner;* The Hoephner Award, poetry, *Southern Humanities Review*; and Poet of the Year, Ohio Poetry Day Association, for *After Oz*.

In 1991 he was named contributing editor for *Writer's Digest* and is responsible each month for a 2000-word column about making and marketing poetry. In 1993 and 1994, he edited the directory *Poet's Market* (Writer's Digest Books). His text *The Art and Craft of Poetry* is used in more than two dozen MFA programs.

Bugeja earned a doctorate in creative writing at Oklahoma State University, a master's degree in mass communication at South Dakota State University, and a bachelor's degree in German at Saint Peter's College. He also has received several teaching honors, including an AMOCO Foundation Outstanding Teacher Award (Oklahoma State University, 1985) and the University Professor Award (Ohio University, 1987).

He is a full professor at the prestigious E.W. Scripps School of Journalism, Ohio University, where he teaches ethics and writing. Before entering academe, Bugeja was state editor for United Press International. Bugeja lives in Athens, Ohio, with his wife Diane and their children Erin and Shane.